# Your Five- and Six-Year-Old

## *As They Grow*

# Your Five- and Six-Year-Old

## *As They Grow*

By the Editors of **Parents** Magazine
and Marge Kennedy

St. Martin's Griffin ⚞ New York

**Also by Parents Magazine:**
The Parents Answer Book
Parents Magazine's It Worked for Me!
The Parents Party Book
Play and Learn
The Parents Book of Lists
Your One-Year-Old: As They Grow
Your Two-Year-Old: As They Grow
Your Three- and Four-Year-Old: As They Grow
I Can Do It!: Physical Milestones for the First Twelve Months
I Can Do It!: Physical Milestones for One-Year-Olds
I Can Do It!: Physical Milestones for Two-Year-Olds
I Can Do It!: Physical Milestones for Three- and Four-Year-Olds

A Roundtable Press Book

**For Roundtable Press, Inc.:**
Directors: Julie Merberg, Marsha Melnick, Susan E. Meyer
Project editor: Meredith Wolf Schizer
Designer: Laura Smyth
Computer production: Carrie Glidden
Illustrator: Penny Carter

**For Parents Magazine:**
Editor in chief: Sally Lee
Deputy editor: Linda Fears
G+J Director of books and licensing: Tammy Palazzo

www.stmartins.com

ISBN 0-312-26419-4

First St. Martin's Griffin Edition: November 2000

D 10 9 8 7 6 5 4 3 2 1

# Contents

Foreword by Sally Lee                                          10

## I love you, now go away!                                    11
### *Your child's need for you versus his need for independence*
Developmental Milestone: Separating from Mom                   14
Conflict: Anger at Mom's loss of power                         16
You and Your Child: How your child's growing independence
  affects your relationship                                    18
 The importance of Dad to your five- and six-year-old     19
 Your child's birth order and his sense of independence   20
Helping Your Child Grow: Nurturing independence                23
 Helping your child define his role in the family
    and community                                    25
 Self-care skills to encourage now                        26
 Activities to enhance your child's comfort with
    independence                                     28

## I'm the best, but someone else is better                    29
### *Your child's sense of self*
Developmental Milestone: Your child's ability to be
  objective about herself                                      31
 Teaching the importance of hard work                     34
 Helping your young perfectionist accept herself          35
Conflict: Maintaining a strong ego in the face of limitations  37
 A word about bed-wetting and accidents                   39
 Physical skills your five- and six-year-old needs to
    master                                           40
 Tips for riding a two-wheeler                            41

You and Your Child: How your own judgments about your
    child affect your relationship    43
        Helping your child appreciate who she is    44
Helping Your Child Grow: Fostering resilience    45

# Ready or not, here I come!   47
### *Your child's school readiness*

Developmental Milestone: School readiness    48
    The emotional and social skills your kindergartner
        needs    49
    The academic skills your kindergartner needs    50
    Preparing your child for kindergarten    51
    The ability to comply with teachers' expectations    52
    What to look for in a kindergarten setting    53
    The kindergarten curriculum    54
    The academic skills kindergarten teachers teach    56
    What your kindergartner's day might be like    57
    The right age for kindergarten    58
Conflict: Frustration with the demands and pace of learning    63
    Easing your child's fear of starting school    64
You and Your Child: Supporting your child's learning    66
Helping Your Child Grow: Developing a partnership with
    your child's teacher    68
    Handling homework    69
    Making the transition to first grade    70

# What I know and how I learn   71
### *Your child's learning style*

Developmental Milestone: Abstract thinking    74
    How your child learns math concepts    76
    Helping your child understand numerical concepts    78
    Your child's understanding of time    79

Conflict: Adapting to classroom experiences that may not
    suit her learning style    81
      Learning disabilities and differences    81
      What to know about attention-deficit disorder (ADD)
        and attention-deficit hyperactivity disorder (ADHD)    83
      Getting a diagnosis of ADD or ADHD    84
You and Your Child: Understanding the connection between
    your and your child's learning styles    85
Helping Your Child Grow: Providing learning opportunities
    tailored to your child's style    86
      Helping your young student get organized    87

# Let me tell you a story    89
### *Your child's reading and writing skills*

Developmental Milestone: Readiness to read    90
      The debate about reading instruction    91
      The strategies new readers use    92
      Reading in the classroom    94
Conflict: The cost of learning to read    95
      Learning to write    97
      Writing in the classroom    97
      The drawing-writing connection    98
You and Your Child: Supporting your child's comfort
    with writing    99
Helping Your Child Grow: Raising a reader    100
      Making the most of reading time    102
      Tips for helping your child read aloud confidently    103
      Recognizing reading difficulties    104

# I am what I am 107
### *Your child's personality and gender identity*

Developmental Milestone: Strong identification with
    same-sex parent 109
Conflict: Pride in and a sense of privacy about her body 110
    Talking to your child about sexuality 111
You and Your Child: Dealing with your child's temperament 113
    Dealing with a sensitive child 114
Helping Your Child Grow: Avoiding gender stereotyping 116

# Who's in charge here? 118
### *Disciplining your child*

Developmental Milestone: Recognizing that families
    have different rules 120
Conflict: Living up to rising expectations 121
You and Your Child: Encouraging positive behavior 122
    Common misbehaviors and how to deal with them 125
Helping Your Child Grow: Useful responses to misbehavior 127
    Handling your own anger 129

# That's not fair! 130
### *Your child's moral development*

Developmental Milestone: An internal sense of right
    and wrong 131
    Teaching your child values 132
    Raising an empathetic child 133
    Helping your child evaluate situations from a
        moral angle 135
    The truth about honesty 136

Conflict: Why isn't everything perfect? 136

You and Your Child: Helping your child develop personal
values 138

Helping Your Child Grow: Helping your child learn from
her mistakes 140

The importance of manners 141

# Keep me safe 142
### *Helping your child avoid harm*

Developmental Milestone: Caution 143

Conflict: Advance and Retreat 143

Car and pedestrian accidents 145

Drowning 147

Fire 148

Playground injuries 150

Sports safety 150

Appliances, tools, and lawnmowers 151

Bunk beds 152

Firearms 152

You and Your Child: Keeping your child safe without
being overprotective 153

Teaching your child about "stranger danger" 154

Dealing with bullies 155

Helping Your Child Grow: Teaching safety rules 156

Respect your child's uniqueness 157

The best books 158

The best videos 159

The best computer programs 160

# Foreword

## by Sally Lee

Welcome to magic time! Though every stage of a child's development is certainly a unique, exciting learning experience for both parent and child, raising five- and six-year-olds is particularly rewarding.

Five-year-olds are full of energy and enthusiasm. They're cheerful, cooperative, eager to please, and even more eager to learn. Six-year-olds exhibit many of the same delightful traits, though they tend to experience more mood swings and more defiant behavior in a quest for greater independence from Mom and Dad. There are many "firsts" that accompany this age: losing the first tooth, joining a sports team, reading aloud, and perhaps the most momentous event in the life of a five- and six-year-old, starting "real" school.

This book will help you celebrate the milestones, encourage burgeoning independence, and weather the rough times. We'll teach you how to hone your child's social skills, boost her self-esteem, gauge her readiness to begin kindergarten, identify her learning style, and give you the tools to practice her reading and writing skills at home. By understanding the various mental, physical, and emotional stages in the development of a five- and six-year-old, you'll be prepared for the many teachable moments that lie ahead—and truly enjoy this exciting stage in your child's life.

# I love you, now go away!

## Your child's need for you versus his need for independence

If you're lucky enough to be the parent of a newly minted five-year-old, get ready to enjoy some of the very best months you'll ever know as a parent. Your just-turned five-year-old is a delightful bundle of smiles and high spirits, an enthusiastic learner, and, perhaps most gratifying, your number-one fan. This is a time when you can do no wrong, when your company and your approval are the things your child treasures most, and, a bit ironically, the age when he's finally independent enough to allow you more time to yourself.

No longer likely to bolt into traffic, your cooperative child seems to have developed an innate sense of his own limitations. The arrival of common sense doesn't leave him uninspired or afraid of the world, however. In fact, it's quite the contrary. His sense of pride at what he can do fuels his ego and inspires his every action. He's incredibly happy to be himself. He's brimming with confidence and can't wait to show you how skilled he can be at anything. Aware of just how much fun it is to be five, some astute five-year-olds may announce, "I want everything to stay the same forever." No doubt, you'll agree.

During this period, you may find yourself accepting compliments about your child's politeness, zest for life, tenacity, and general good will. Rightly, you feel great pride for raising such a terrific kid. Then, when you least expect it, the light of your life seems to get caught under a storm cloud. His sunny disposition turns bleak. He's angry at you because you didn't know that he didn't want his usual tuna sandwich for lunch today. Instead of the hug and kiss you expected to receive after a brief separation, he may turn on his heel, rejecting any sign of affection from you when you pick him up from a playdate. Rather than proudly presenting you with his latest artistic creation for you to hang on the fridge, he may tear up his drawing, declaring that his work is "ugly" or "dumb." What happened?

Rest assured, it's nothing you've done. It's just that your five-year-old, so recently convinced of your perfection, is furious to find out that you're not as in tune with him as he assumed or as powerful as he imagined. You can't read his mind, anticipate his needs, and make everything okay. He reasons that if you aren't as all-powerful as he thought, then perhaps, he, too, is not as in control as he believed.

At five, your child is also likely to be experiencing a bit of social pressure to grow up and move away from you emotionally. He's probably starting kindergarten, an experience vastly different from the comfort of nursery school. He senses that the demands on him are different than in the past.

In the few months you had to enjoy his model behavior as a new five-year-old, you've grown accustomed to depending on his cooperation. It's easy to forget during this blissful time that your five-year-old still has a long way to go toward maturity. His ability to control his impulses has not, in fact, arrived fully developed. It, like his body, is merely reorganizing: He hasn't yet mastered the ability to understand and control his emotions or his physical actions consistently. He increasingly understands that neither he nor you really run the universe. But he's not sure who's in charge.

To top it off, his body is rapidly changing. His baby teeth are falling out, and he's teething again. His sleep and eating patterns are going through a change, too. Between five and six, he'll grow three inches or more and put on weight, making him hungrier and more tired than he was at the brink of age five. The growth spurt triggers a temporary return to the clumsiness of his toddler years, as he struggles to get used to a world in which the chairs are not so big and he can easily reach the light switch. His association with more kids at school will result in more colds and general malaise as he picks up every bug going around.

Between the ages of about five-and-a-half and six-and-a-half, your child is once again a jumble of contrary feelings like he was in his earlier preschool days. One minute, he loves you passionately. The next, he hates you because it's raining and he wants to play outside. At five, he's thrilled and proud to be heading off to school, sure you'll be as happy to see him as he is to see you at the end of the day. A few months later, he may be terrified that you won't be there when school gets out. Entering the age of five, he's acutely aware of all of his talents and capabilities. Moving toward six, he's equally aware that he's not the best at everything. The swing back toward feelings of self-confidence and approval of you takes place as your child approaches age seven, when he'll once again show you the calm, cooperative behavior you enjoyed when he first turned five. In the meantime, it helps to remind yourself not to take your child's mood swings too personally.

## DEVELOPMENTAL MILESTONE
## Separating from Mom

Since infancy, and especially during the toddler years, your child has been experimenting with inching away from you, testing himself—and you—to see just how far he could venture safely. At age four, he may have defiantly set out to put distance between himself and you, demanding more freedom than you reasonably could allow.

At five, he knows he's proven to himself and to you that he really is a separate person, capable of so much. He can play in a room by himself without your constant supervision. He can entertain friends without nonstop surveillance. He can go off to school and return full of new ideas about himself and the world. The payoff for all this independence is his ability to return to you and report on his day, to show off what he's done, and to share with you what he's learned. His brimming confidence in himself is matched only by his brimming confidence in you. At this moment, he's not only content to be cooperative, he feels secure in knowing that he's capable of abiding by your will. He loves showing you how good he is at being good.

The change that takes place in the middle of the fifth year is not a blatant desire to be uncooperative or disobedient. Rather it's a need to experiment with taking the next step away from you. With a reserve of total trust in you, your child is willing to risk your anger and your disappointment for the payoff of proving that he's even more capable than you think he is. He might, for example, attempt to show you how he can swim by diving off the deep end of a pool, whether or not he's really able to stay above the waterline. A less adventurous child might try to clear the dinner dishes to show how helpful he can be. He might expect compliments for his actions, even when they defy your spelled-out rules and even when the results are clearly (even to him) not good.

He'll experiment with misbehaviors to learn just how powerful you are, too. For instance, he might fib, not solely out of a desire to avoid taking responsibility for doing something wrong, but to test whether you're really able to discern the truth. Can you really peek inside his head and know what he's thinking? Can you really be sure that he broke the lamp if you didn't witness it crashing to the floor? The information that he gathers from your reactions to him and his behavior confirms to him that you really are a person separate from him. The scary counterpart to this realization is that if you cannot know all there is about him and his needs, then he is more alone in the world than he previously believed. His reaction may be to cling to you rather than to accept that ultimately you and he must remain separate. But this clinginess, and your reaction to it, can set off a cycle of neediness, and anger with himself over that neediness. A moment after grasping your hand, he may feel compelled to stomp away from you, venting a string of complaints about your shortcomings.

# How it feels to be me

I really love being a big kid. Now I can do so many things that babies and little kids can't do. I know all of the words to my favorite songs, and I can play games with my friends without grown-ups telling us what to do all the time. I like thinking about things and figuring out how things work. I can read, and I like to make up stories to go with the pictures. I love school. I love the smell of my pencil case. It's important to me to be good and to act like a big kid so that no one thinks I'm still little.

I miss being able to cuddle up in Mommy's lap all the time. Now she tells me that I'm too big to carry, even when I'm tired. Sometimes I wish I was little again and didn't have to know so much. It was more fun in nursery school. Now I have to sit still a lot and do things like write my name and find my own pencils and put on my own jacket. I'm tired. Why can't there be more nap time in school? Why do I have to learn letters and try to read to myself? Why can't Mommy read everything to me like she used to? If I could, I'd go back to being a little kid for a while. But I'll wait until after I learn to ride a two-wheeler.

The best way to weather the storms that swirl around and through your five- or six-year-old is to enjoy the sunny days and to recognize that during the other moments, your child is every bit as confused by his behavior as you are. Realize that, though it might not seem so, your child remains terribly concerned about pleasing you and earning your approval. The independence that he's stumbling toward now will eventually allow you both to enjoy each other from a more mature perspective.

## CONFLICT
# Anger at Mom's loss of power

When your child turned five, he was secure in both his powers and yours. If something went wrong, he knew he could turn to you for comfort. Even if your response was to urge him to work out his difficulties on his own, the simple fact of checking in with you gave him the security he needed to recover from his hurt. If you held him close and soothed him rather than sending him off to find his own solution to his problem, well, that was okay, too. After all, it bought him more time and attention from you. Whatever you did, whatever you recommended—that was the right thing.

Sometime during his move toward six and continuing until he's nearly seven, your child becomes aware that neither you nor he can wholly control his world. When you prod him to work out a problem on his own, he may react with anger. He feels abandoned, adrift, unloved. If, instead, you offer unrestrained comfort, you still risk his anger. "I need my mother too much!" he thinks. His inner drive to mature, mixed with his natural immaturity, causes him to push away from you even while crying for the comfort of your lap. He'll spend the next year or so working out this dilemma.

During this period, your child's behavior often calls out for correction. He may dawdle over homework, have a temper tantrum when it's time to go to bed, or be out-and-out defiant. Unlike the toddler, who misbehaves in order to test his limits, your misbehaving five-and-a-half to six-and-a-half-year-old often does so to test your love. If you're not as powerful as you once were, perhaps your love isn't as strong either, he fears.

The fear of losing your approval and, thus, your love, is strong now. It doesn't take much to push the buttons of your child's insecurity. If, for example, you ask him to hold his pencil correctly while writing his name, he may think that you love him less for his inability to remember how to hold a pencil. If you ask him to do something that he doesn't want to do, he may blow up at your failure to recognize what he has recently recognized—the fact that you don't really control him. However, after an outburst, even one in which he loudly declares that he hates you, he may ask plaintively, "Are you mad at me?" or, "Do you still love me?"

Your power to make everything okay hasn't really gone away. But it has changed from the simplistic kissing away of a boo-boo to a more complex ritual. Now, your child tests the limits of your separateness. How far can he pull away from you before you rein him in? Can you still love him completely even when he's "bad"? Can you feel the same angry, even hateful, feelings toward him that he can feel for you? Is your love for him just as overwhelming to you as his love is for you? Do you have the same need to get away from him that he sometimes has to get away from you? Would you ever act on those feelings? Would you ever leave him? He cannot, even to himself, articulate these fears—so he acts them out instead.

As this stage in your child's life, he is moving from a total trust in the power of your love, to an insecurity about the bond you share, eventually to a more reasoned idea that, in spite of his imperfections (and yours), your love is a constant. By the age of seven, if you provide him with the reassurance that, though you may not always approve of his actions, you nevertheless always love him, his volatile mood swings will diminish. He will accept your limitations as well as his own more readily. He will understand that your inability to comprehend everything and do everything for him does not lessen your love for him, or his for you.

# How your child's growing independence affects your relationship

When your child insists on buttoning his own sweater rather than accepting your help, the motive is definitely to show off to you how big he's become. No matter that the buttons don't line up quite right. He's still anxious to strut before you, showing off his accomplishment. Your approval and acknowledgment of this feat means the world to him. He's not just proud of himself. He's proud of your pride in him.

A few months later, at five-and-a-half, he may decide that putting on his own sweater is too much work. "I caaaan't!" he might moan, thrusting it into your hands so that you can help him. Or he may decide that, in spite of the chill in the air, he doesn't need his "dumb sweater." It's easier, after all, not to bother trying than to risk buttoning it incorrectly. It's hard to know whether you should offer to help or not. Either way, you'll be wrong.

Don't be surprised, however, if your five-and-a-half to six-and-a-half-year-old turns to your spouse for help or willingly accepts a teacher's or older child's assistance with grace. What's going on? Simply, it's okay for your child to lean on others for help. It's just from you that he needs his freedom.

While busily rejecting your involvement in his life much of the time, your child is now happily forging relationships with others. Dad becomes extremely important at this stage, as do teachers and big kids. You'll be rebuked with statements like, "My teacher doesn't do it that way," when you offer homework help. This is the age, too, when your child learns to play one parent against the other with finesse. If, for instance, you deny your child a cookie before dinner, he'll simply wander over to his other parent and ask, "Can I have a cookie?" He'll see no need to mention that you already said no.

How should you react to your child's seeming rejection at times? Most importantly, don't take it too seriously. Remember that your child is not really rejecting *you*. He's rejecting his *dependence* on you. He uses others as a yardstick to measure the importance of your relationship. And he's hedging his bets. If, as he sometimes fears, he could lose your love, he's making sure that there are others around who will care for him in case you don't.

Your reactions to his many mood swings lay the groundwork for how your relationship develops over the next few years. Too much coddling and you risk convincing him that he's incapable of being apart from you. Too little attention leaves him with exaggerated fears of abandonment. Too much correction of his misbehaviors may encourage outright defiance or quiet complacency in an effort to please. Too little discipline leaves your child feeling frightened and alone, unsure of what is expected of him. Clearly, it's a fine line you'll have to walk during this period of your child's life.

### The importance of Dad to your five- and six-year-old

From infancy on, your child has been acutely aware of his dad's "otherness." He knows that Dad responds differently to his questions, holds him in a different way, plays differently, is perhaps more physical and less verbal with him.

Now this "otherness" serves your child especially well. Dad provides another loving parent. But while your child may have once pulled away from Dad and toward Mom for comfort when he was upset, now the pull is more toward Dad. Dad provides another way of looking at the world and offers a different kind of comfort. His kisses and hugs are not only a great sign of his love, but they assure your child that his goodness and worth are seen and valued by someone other than Mom. A word of praise from Dad becomes a trophy of sorts. Mom's love, after all, is seen as unconditional. Dad's approval is earned, and that's a significant difference.

An active and positively involved dad is a boost to both a boy's and a girl's sense of identity and self-esteem. Boys and girls both learn from Dad what it means to be male, something even the best mom can't teach. They learn how to handle emotional, intellectual, and physical challenges in ways that are likely to differ somewhat from Mom's way of doing things. They learn that there is more than one way to approach problems, more than one way to interact with the world. Between what they've learned from Mom and what they're studying now about Dad, they can find their own way to act in relation to ideas and to people. Most importantly, Dad lets your child move away from you while maintaining the closeness and security of family.

## Your child's birth order and his sense of independence

Your child's innate personality has at least as much to do with how he approaches issues surrounding independence as does his birth order. *(For more on personality, see pages 107–17.)* Nevertheless, each child's placement within the family does contribute somewhat to how much or how little independence he demands and how well he handles the independence he's granted. The following can help you understand your child's quest for independence from a birth-order perspective:

*First-borns and only children.* Kids who enjoy the focused attention of their parents during infancy, as most first-borns and onlies do, are more oriented toward adults than they are to other children. Their social and emotional development is patterned on grown-ups. Doting parents of firsts and onlies tend to encourage and applaud each step toward individualism that their infants and toddlers exhibit. This encouragement extends into the preschool and school years, as parents respond with delight to their child's every accomplishment. Overall, first-borns develop a sense of independence with more confidence and less emotional turbulence than do other children.

Onlies, if given lots of encouragement, also accept the challenges of independence more readily than do later children. However, if onlies are overly protected, they learn to distrust their quest for independence. With a strong bond between you, your only child may be more anxious than either first-borns or later arrivals and may also be anxious about leaving you alone as he takes the necessary steps toward independence. In order to achieve the separateness he needs, he may become particularly defiant, almost egging you on to push him away so that he doesn't have to take on all the responsibility for pulling away from you himself.

*Your first born as an older sibling.* When first-borns become older siblings, they not only retain their privileged position, their status tends to grow as they become a sort of standard bearer by which parents measure all subsequent children. Even at a fairly young age, a first-born might be depended upon somewhat to assist in the child-rearing of his younger siblings, sometimes only by example. First-borns, then, naturally develop a sense of entitlement regarding their parents' affection and approval. They expect to be leaders, and they usually are. They are likely, however, to resent the intrusion of later kids on their parents' time and attention. When they become siblings before age five, this resentment can cause them to attempt to regress to an earlier time when they had you all to themselves.

When your child becomes an older sibling at the age of five, most resentment takes a back seat to feelings of joy at becoming a big sib. He is likely to strut like a proud new parent, eager to show the new baby what it means to be part of the family. He's anxious to help out: he'll tip-toe around to show you how good he can be at not waking the baby, and he'll happily "read" to or show the baby all the things he can do. If the new baby arrives when he's five-and-a-half to six-and-a-half, however, he's more likely to be put off balance by the event. He may misbehave, too, if that works to divert your attention away from the baby and back to him.

As the older sibling of a toddler or preschooler, your five- or six-year-old child will enjoy his role as a mentor to his younger sister or brother. He will, however, expect you to protect his things from his younger siblings and to keep them away when he's playing with his friends.

***Your five- and six-year-old as a middle child.*** Middle children never enjoy the unique position of first-borns, but many, of course, spend time as the baby of the family. Growing up, a middle child is often acutely aware of his uneasy status within the family. He's neither the oldest, who rates special privileges, nor the youngest, who requires a different kind of attention. More needy of parents' reassurance that he does indeed hold a special place in the family, your middle child is more likely than his siblings to be rebellious. After all, his rebellion sets him apart from his other, and in his mind favored, siblings.

***Your middle-child five- and six-year-old as an older sibling.*** Like a first-born, a middle child whose family expands when he's five will take great pride in the new arrival. He'll claim the newborn as his own, a position he feels is his right, as if, finally, you've done something really special for him. He assumes he's better at the job of being a sibling than any other kids in the family might be. It's all part of his glowing confidence in himself right now.

Your five-and-a-half to six-and-a-half-year-old, however, may actually ignore the birth, treating a new baby as an inconvenience and not much else. This, however, is true only if other aspects of his life are running somewhat smoothly. If he's just started school, or if you've just moved, or if he's having difficulties with his friends for any reason, the new baby might represent one more blow to his shaky self-esteem. "I'm being replaced!" he fears with an urgency even more pronounced than he might have felt as a toddler.

***Your five- and six-year-old as a youngest child.*** Less anxious than first-borns to please their parents and with a more secure position in the family than middle-borns, youngest children look to their older sibs for information about the family as much as they look to Mom and Dad—sometimes even more. Like oldest children, they intuit that they have a special relationship with you and that they deserve special privileges. Unlike oldest kids in a family, they also have a sibling or two or more to act as a buffer between themselves and you. For attention, they can turn to you or to an older sibling with an almost equal desire for connection. They do not compete for your attention the way oldest and middle children do. They expect it when they want it, but can also be satisfied with a brother or sister's attention.

The shift in behavior between a happy-go-lucky five and a moody five-and-a-half to six-year-old holds true for your youngest child in most ways. But in matters of independence, your youngest child will have more difficulty separating from you. Very possibly, he'll be more clingy and less mature than others his age. As he heads off to school or even to an afternoon visit with Grandma, he may beg you to stay and become inconsolate when you can't. Like others his age, he will adapt and forge ahead. But it will probably be a more emotional experience for him.

## HELPING YOUR CHILD GROW
## Nurturing independence

Your five- and six-year-old is on the cusp of something great. He's taking his first big steps into the world outside, a world full of challenges that may be scary at first, but ones that he's anxious to meet. To help support his desire and his need to grow in independence:

*Respect your child's individuality.* Throughout his childhood, it's important for your child to know that you love him just for who he is. He may not be as proficient at reading as his big sister was at this age; he may be noisier and less focused than his friend; he may have interests in things that don't appeal to you. Whoever he is, however, he needs to know that you cherish the unique aspects of his personality, looks, and feelings that make him who he is. Make a point now and again of complimenting the things that are special about him. But since being like you is one of his goals right now, don't go overboard in delineating how he differs from you.

***Encourage social skills.*** The five- and six-year-old who's comfortable meeting new people, who can handle himself appropriately at social events, and who can, in general, behave in public, garners a terrific sense of pride at being regarded as a big kid. Since this is an age when he wants so very much to please you, instilling social graces now—reminding him to say "please" and "thank you," for example—will be easier than it was in your child's younger years. Hearing your and others' praises for his good behavior will further encourage this kind of mature behavior, which, in turn, makes your child less anxious about being out of your line of vision and on his own.

***Present age-appropriate responsibilities.*** As recently as age four, your child "helped" you with chores around the house. At five and six, he can be given meaningful responsibility that contributes to his and the family's well-being. Chores such as making his bed and clearing the table every day are actions that are relatively easy to carry out and include the big payoff of earning your sincere thanks for a job well done.

***Let your child make reasonable choices.*** Each evening, have your child pick out his clothes for school the next day rather than depending on you to make the fashion selections. Making such choices encourages other self-care skills such as getting dressed. Likewise, let him contribute to family decisions about the daily menu, especially his school lunch, and choosing what movie you and he might see on the weekend. Don't, however, extend his choices into areas that you can't live with. For example, don't give him carte blanche to choose an inappropriate TV program; limit the choices he can make to a range of good options. And when he makes his selection from within the acceptable range, be sure to show your approval.

*Insist on an age-appropriate level of self-care.* After years of tying his shoes and supervising tooth-brushing, it can be hard to pull back and let your child struggle to do the things he must do on his own. But continuing to do for him what he can and should be doing for himself is a real disservice to your child. Adjust your schedule and your standards to allow him time to take care of himself in ways that he should.

## Helping your child define his role in the family and community

Your child knows that your family and community are special. He's glad now to be part of both and wouldn't trade places with someone else for the world. Being part of such a great group has a status all its own. Having some defined jobs within the family and the community enhances that status. While no five- or six-year-old can reasonably be expected to handle the responsibility for running any aspect of the household independently, your child can have prescribed tasks that let him know he's making a meaningful contribution to the family's welfare. When choosing chores for your child, avoid gender stereotypes. Be sure to encourage your son to help out in the kitchen and your daughter in the garage. Some chores that five- and six-year-olds can reasonably assume:

*Pet care.* Your child can make sure that the dog's water bowl is washed and refilled daily or that the parakeet's food dish is full. Do not, however, expect a child this age to assume most of the responsibility for any pet.

*Meal preparation and cleanup.* Your child can make the salad, stir ingredients (away from a stove), or help to set the table. Be sure to thank him for his assistance.

*Laundry help.* A five- or six-year-old can sort dark and light colors and help fold items such as washcloths and towels as well as match socks before putting them away.

*Daily or weekly housecleaning.* Choose an aspect of housekeeping that doesn't involve chemicals or electric appliances for your child to do, such as damp-cloth dusting, stacking newspapers, rinsing bottles for recycling, or watering plants.

*Seasonal housekeeping.* Have your child go through his clothes to find outgrown items for donation to charity or for storage for younger sibs. Let him wash old toys for giving away or for a yard sale.

*Spiritual involvement.* Encourage your child to lead grace at the table or to partake in religious services in ways that your congregation deems appropriate for children his age.

*Community activity.* Take your child to playground cleanups, holiday gift gathering for the needy, or other meaningful work to benefit the neighborhood.

## Self-care skills to encourage now
It's important that while your child now be encouraged to perform certain self-care activities, he continues to feel appropriately "babied" with all the hugs and kisses he still wants and needs. Being able to take care of the following will not only increase his sense of competence, but will go a long way toward helping him develop the social skills he needs now.

*Dressing.* Your child should be getting himself dressed by now. To make the process easier, choose easy-on-and-off clothes with easy-to-use fasteners—zippers with big pulls, large buttons, working snaps, and so on. If shoelaces are proving too difficult right now, get shoes with Velcro closures or slip-ons so that he gets out of the habit of placing his foot before you for lacing. Don't put off learning to tie a bow too long, however, as it becomes very hard to find shoes larger than a size 2 with Velcro.

***Bathing.*** It still makes sense for you to fill your child's bath or to make sure that the shower is set at the right temperature. However, your five- and six-year-old is ready for a bit of privacy and independence as he bathes. He may still need you to wash and rinse his hair as well. *Note: Don't stray far when your five- or six-year-old is alone in the bath. Also, teach him never to touch the faucets, which could lead to scalding.*

***Caring for his own room.*** Keep his linens simple and teach your child how to make his own bed. It's essential that you learn to live with the possibly crooked results if you are to encourage him to make this task a habit. At five and six, your child should also be responsible for general straightening up of his space, including putting dirty laundry in the hamper and putting toys and books where they belong.

***Tending to his own sports and play gear.*** By now, it should be up to your child to gather and carry the gear he wants or needs to play in the park or on sports teams. (Exceptions can be made for very heavy equipment such as ice-hockey gear.) He should also be responsible for keeping track of his gear and for regular upkeep, such as putting his bike away after riding.

***Caring for his own school equipment.*** Remind your child to check that he's packed his homework and sharpened pencils for the next day—and that he's given you any papers he may have brought home from school for you, but don't pack his bag or rummage through it for him.

**Activities to enhance your child's comfort with independence**
Being independent can bring a sense of loss to your child as well as gains. It's therefore important that his experience with independence involves some fun, not just work. To help entice your child to move toward appropriate independence:

*Ask his opinion.* Being invited into an adult conversation is a real ego-booster. When discussing something that your child can be privy to and in which he's likely to have some stake—such as whether or not he likes the new playground design—encourage him to add his two cents' worth. Don't be dismissive of his ideas even if they seem outlandish to you.

*Share in responsibilities.* Doing things on his own can be lonely. Join your child as he completes his chores, maybe helping him make his bed. Sit at the table paying bills while he does his homework.

*Consider giving an allowance.* By the age of five, your child knows that money is important. Give him a regular allowance and help him learn how to spend and save wisely. Also give him opportunities to earn extra money for big jobs. Don't, however, bribe him with cash or toys for doing what's expected of him.

*Don't overwhelm him with responsibilities.* Even if your child seems capable of handling chores and homework and self-care with relative ease, keep his age and maturity level in mind. Don't expect him to take on too much or to perform tasks at an older child's level of competence. Never put your five- or six-year-old in charge of a younger sibling, for instance. While your kindergartner or first-grader may be a great companion for your younger child, and may be helpful to you in keeping the younger one busy for a few moments at a time, he simply is not ready to be a baby-sitter.

# I'm the best, but someone else is better

## Your child's sense of self

At the cusp of age five, there seems to be no limit to what your child can do.

Her body has matured so that it more closely resembles an older child's. Her arms and legs are more muscular. Now she probably skips, hops on one foot, and climbs ladders with ease. She's matured intellectually, too. Though she still spends a lot of time in fantasy play, she's beginning to grasp the difference between make-believe and reality. And with a growing vocabulary and better use of grammar, she's able to express herself more fluidly.

Socially, your child is increasingly interested in being with other children, even if that means separating from you more. Her play style begins to take on gender-stereotypical form. Your daughter will likely be more drawn to doing things she deems feminine and to playing more with other girls. Similarly, your son will show a marked preference for whatever he deems to be boyish. He may refuse to play with girls at all, especially if there are boys around.

While home and family were once the focus of your child's world, they now become a refuge of sorts from her other encounters. A smile, a hug, a reassuring word from you—these things can act as insulation against the harsh winds of the outside world. The reverse is also true: Showing your disappointment or disapproval, even though sometimes you must, hits your child particularly hard at this age.

During the ages of five and six, more and more people enter your child's orbit, and their opinions and reactions begin to count, too. Now, not only is your child concerned about your love and attention, she's looking to see how her teacher responds to her and what her friends have to say about her. And she's thinking that growing up is becoming increasingly challenging and frustrating, even while being exciting and fun. She understands that a lot is required of her. And for the most part, she's willing and able to meet the challenge.

In addition to "being good," something she continually strives to be, your kindergartner or first-grader has to be "good at" certain things now. If she's in school, she's expected to sit still and pay attention to things that may or may not interest her. Counting numbers, naming the days of the week, learning to wait her turn, stand in line, or raise her hand for attention—the list of requirements may seem endless to her. Perhaps most important, she's expected to unravel the mysteries of the written language, learning how to read and write. *(For more on this important skill, see pages 89–106.)*

The playground doesn't offer any relief to your maturing five- and six-year-old's conflicting feelings about growing up. Where so recently it was the place your child could revel in unlimited imaginative and physical play, she's now much more aware of what the other kids are doing—and how they're judging her. She may be able to pump herself on the swings now; but whereas she used to close her eyes tightly and make believe that she was flying, now she opens her eyes and notices that the kid on the next swing is soaring higher. While her trike or two-wheeler with training wheels once carried her proudly, she may now hear snickers from the other kids: "Look, she still has *training* wheels!" At five, the sneer won't trouble her. At six, however, she may suddenly feel ashamed of what is supposed to be fun.

For many, if not most, children, this period brings on mixed reactions. One day she may burst into tears when she realizes she can't do everything she wants to. Another day, she may simply focus on learning what she decides is important to her. Your child is, indeed, thrilled when she meets the challenges set before her. The interim moments when she struggles, however, are hard on her—and on you. Your job now is to help her achieve what she must with her ego intact.

## DEVELOPMENTAL MILESTONE
## Your child's ability to be objective about herself
Kids five and younger are happy to remove themselves emotionally from competition. Playing—just being there—is what counts. They don't expect to be able to do certain "big kid" things like read, so they don't feel bad if they can't. As she approaches five- to five-and-a-half, your child naturally sheds the insulation that has, thus far, protected her strong ego. She may react to the need to learn new things by drawing closer to home, wanting to spend more time with you, where she feels safe and competent. Or she may be determined to go about mastering the skills that she believes she needs now. More likely she'll waver, spending some energy on boosting her achievements and then taking breaks in your lap to recharge her mental and emotional batteries.

With a wider circle of social contacts, she begins to measure herself and her family against others. She may be startled to find out that not every family does things just as yours does. At five, she'll be convinced that your way is the best way and will have no problem telling another mom that "At my house, we never drink soda with dinner. Drinking soda is bad." By six, she'll come home and declare, "Why can't we have soda at dinner? Not having soda is a stupid rule." Not all of her evaluations will be negative, though; mostly, she'll continue to judge her own family as superior to others.

Her sense of identity develops to encompass her own accomplishments measured against those of others. While as a new five-year-old she may be content to know that "I'm a fast runner," as a five-and-a-half-year old, she may add, "I can run faster than Will, but not as fast as Samantha." For most kids, learning that they're not the best at everything is okay, provided that each finds something particular about herself to feel proud about. Some, however, retreat, at least temporarily, to babyish behavior rather than moving ahead boldly. Others become perfectionists, driving themselves to accomplish everything well and becoming angry and fearful when they don't. *(For ideas on handling perfectionism, see pages 35–37.)*

The ability to see herself objectively has its risks, however, because the skill is now in its most embryonic stage. Your child's objectivity may, in fact, slip into self-deprecation on occasion. A small disappointment, such as being corrected on the spelling of a word, can go from "I made a mistake" to "I'm not a good speller" to "I'm a bad speller" to "I'm a bad person" in mere seconds. Clearly the objectivity a five-and-a-half or six-year-old can feel doesn't include the ability to balance the disappointment with reminders that she is a good friend or that she's great at adding numbers. That's where you come in. Reassurance along with practical support to help your child attain her goals goes a long way to keeping her self-evaluations in perspective.

| If your child... | Do say | Don't say |
|---|---|---|
| says, "I'll never learn to ride a two-wheeler." | "That's hard for a lot of kids your age. Let's find some extra time to practice this weekend." | "I don't know why. All the other kids seem to be getting it." |
| comes in third in a race | "You ran really well." | "Why didn't you try harder? You could have won," **or** "Don't feel bad about not winning." |
| boasts that she's the best artist in her class | "That's great!" | "If only you'd put as much effort into reading as you do into art, you'd be a good student," **or** "It's not nice to brag." |
| isn't invited to a classmate's birthday party | "It's hard to be left out." Then help her see the possible reasons, such as not really being one of the celebrant's close friends. | "Well, we won't invite her to your party, either," **or** "You don't need to be invited to every party." |
| shows fear about a new activity, such as starting school | "It can be hard to try something new. Let's visit the school so you can get a better idea of what it will be like." | "Stop being a baby." |

## Teaching the importance of hard work

As a preschooler and early five-year-old, your child wore all the trappings of power and position with ease, turning a towel into a superhero's cape or a hairband into a tiara. She easily adopted the identity of whomever and whatever she wanted to be. She could readily pretend that she could fly, grant wishes, or climb Mount Everest. Though she will continue to enjoy this sort of fantasy play through the age of eight or so, something else is taking hold. She'll find that she needs to contribute not only imagination, but hard work, toward accomplishing the skills and identities she imagines she has.

This reality can be traumatic for some children. If she wants to learn to play an instrument, for example, she may be astounded to find out that simply banging on the keys isn't enough. When her letters don't look as straight as the ones in her practice book, your five- or six-year-old may simply want to give up. "I can't!" may replace the exuberant "I can!" of just a few months past.

You will do your child a huge service now by helping her to understand the payoff of hard work toward achieving a goal. Begin by reminding her of things she has already accomplished. Retell stories about when she was a baby and learned to walk, how she struggled and practiced, and how all that work made her such a good runner today. Unearth some saved scribbles and let her see for herself how her hours of drawing led from those primitive scrawls to her museum-worthy pieces now. Let her know that you have confidence in her ability to master the task at hand. But be sure to add that she's got to put in time and energy, too. Don't ask her to learn something new entirely on her own—unless, of course, she wants to. Offer the tools and the time to assist her. Compliment her efforts as well as her triumphs. And, most important, be sure not to demand that she master a skill that is simply beyond her development right now. Trying hard and failing, through no fault of her own, will make your child much more reluctant to take on age-appropriate challenges.

### Helping your young perfectionist accept herself

It's not always easy to recognize that a child is a perfectionist. Many perfectionists appear to be models of good behavior, seemingly able to accomplish whatever is put before them. Others show their frustration easily and want to quit anything that appears to be difficult. Some strive to become extremely good at one thing, ignoring or resisting involvement with other activities. One thing all perfectionists share is undue stress. That stress may be self-induced as a product of your child's innate personality, or it may be superimposed by your or another important adult's high expectations. No matter how a child comes to be a perfectionist, she needs help to alleviate her performance anxiety. If your child shows signs of perfectionism:

*Acknowledge her feelings.* Let your perfectionist know that you're aware that she's frustrated or too hard on herself. Give her the opportunity to tell you why she feels she needs to be better than she is. Assure her that honest effort will produce good (and good enough) results. Ask her for examples of perfect people, and help her see that those she perceives as better than she is are perhaps not perfect after all. There's no need to disparage others, but gently point out that a "perfect" classmate who can write each letter without mistakes may not be as accomplished a soccer player as your child is.

*Make sure your child has down time.* Many children come to believe that to please you they must perform well at every activity on their schedule. Cut back on organized activities and let your child have time to do nothing at all.

*Don't criticize or offer unsolicited suggestions.* If your child is doing her work in a competent manner, don't suggest that she add a chimney to her drawing of a house to make it "better" or make a negative comment about her formation of an "A." Let her work be hers. Offer constructive criticism only when asked or when she's attempting to learn something new.

**Don't overpraise.** A child who hears constant praise may be afraid to take chances with a new activity for fear of doing something that's less than praiseworthy.

**Accept failures.** It may be hard to stand back and watch your child struggle and fail. But it's important to allow her to experience failure and to learn from it.

**Acknowledge your own imperfections.** Though your child is busy learning that you, in fact, have faults, it helps to be up-front about them with your perfectionist. Note that you made a mistake

# How it feels to be me

Today I got to hand out the paper in class. That means my teacher really likes me. I felt special having such an important job to do. I hope I get to pass out the paper again. At recess, my friends and I played tag. I liked being "it" at first, but when I couldn't tag everyone else, I got mad and wouldn't play anymore. I'm not good at tag. I won't play it ever again.

All of my friends and I are collecting sports cards. I love my cards. I like showing them to my friends and looking at their cards, too. Little kids don't have collections, but now that I'm big I can do things with other kids and be just like them. I wore a red hat today. A kid in second grade said that red is a dumb color so I can't wear my red hat tomorrow. Red is a dumb color.

I'm the best kicker on my soccer team. My coach said so. On Saturday I will kick the ball all the way into the goal. I'll win the game. My friends will all like me for kicking the ball so well. I hope the other team all gets sick and can't kick on Saturday.

on a report this week at work. Don't burden your child with your problems, of course, but do use an example from your own life to let her know that you survived a mistake—and that making one is not the end of the world.

## CONFLICT
# Maintaining a strong ego in the face of limitations
Your child, quite naturally, wants to feel good about herself, and, for the most part, she does. But as the demands on her become more complex, so do her feelings about herself. She begins to confuse "good at" and "good" when judging herself. In other words, if she's "good at" something, then she's "good." Conversely, being "bad at" something reflects on her "bad" character.

As she busily goes about the task of learning new things, her self-perception rides a see-saw—one minute she's up, convinced that she's good and all is right with the world, and the next, she's down, and when faced with a frustration or disappointment, she deems herself unworthy.

Her drive to accept herself is strong, however. If she's generally secure in her knowledge that you accept and love her, she'll do all that she can to assure you that she is, in fact, the wonderful child you think she is. That may involve working very hard to reach a goal. Or it may require her to step back and decide that she's not ready for a certain challenge. You'll have to help her decide realistically if she should, indeed, forgo certain activities or if she'll need extra help, from you or others, to reach her potential. To help your child develop a strong sense of self:

*Never compare*. The fact that your child may be advanced or lagging in certain areas compared to her friends or siblings is simply part of who she is right now. Comparisons with others only make your child question her abilities if she's lagging, or worry about losing her special status if others should catch up.

**Watch out for labels.** Even positive labels can limit your child's sense of worthiness rather than expand it. So, instead of saying, "You're nice," say, "What you did was nice." In this way, your child feels more in control, knowing that it's her actions that garner approval (or disapproval), not something about her intrinsic self.

**Offer help without making your child feel helpless.** For example, if your child is afraid to learn to swim, allow her the time she needs to sit by the poolside. When she's ready to get into the water, hold her or let her hold on to the sides. Encourage each next step. Work with her to become proficient, particularly in areas that will allow her to interact more fully with her peers. Consider obtaining lessons in skills that your child wants or needs to master.

**Offer assurances.** It's perfectly normal for some kids to be reticent about investigating new activities, such as swimming, or to have difficulty with a skill such as reading. Always let your child know that you're sure she will eventually develop the ability. Never reprimand her or try to shame her for any reluctance to try an activity she deems scary or to achieve something she finds difficult.

**Praise efforts as well as accomplishments.** Your child is now trying to do and learn a lot. Never berate her for her failure to live up to your own or others' expectations, especially when she's making an effort to learn something new. Remind her that hard work and repeated attempts are likely to result in the success she wants. Congratulate her for getting back on the two-wheeler, even after scraping her knee.

**Resist the urge to overpraise.** Empty compliments handed out in an effort to make a child feel good about herself usually have the opposite effect. By five, your child is savvy enough to know whether any action or effort is praiseworthy. Receiving unearned praise makes your child doubt not only her own abilities, but you, too.

## A word about bed-wetting and accidents

Having control over her bodily functions is a sure sign to your child that she's ready to take on the harder task of controlling her emotions. When children beyond the preschool years, however, have a bed-wetting accident, they feel that they've lost control of their bodies and thus can feel shame and fear. A child may wonder, "What's wrong with me?" Just as her emotional development is urging her to venture into the world, she may draw close to home, afraid that she could have a public accident.

It's important to reassure your child that nearly all kids her age have an occasional bed-wetting incident. Treat the event as if it's no big deal (which it isn't). In a matter-of-fact way, involve your child in the clean up. Talk about why these accidents usually occur—overtiredness, drinking too much before bedtime without making an extra bathroom stop, or perhaps a recent stressful event. If bed-wetting is chronic, help your child by sharing these facts with her:

♦ About 15 percent of seven-year-olds regularly wet the bed. Knowing that she's not the only first-grader with this problem can help your child tremendously.

♦ When bed-wetting persists, the cause is almost always an immature or undersized bladder.

Chronic bed-wetting is not in your child's control. Punishment makes the problem worse by compounding a physical problem with an emotional one. (No parent, after all, would punish a child for being shorter than average or for having blue eyes.) Most chronic bed-wetters outgrow the problem without any intervention. As their bladders grow, they gain the ability to hold more urine and to last the night without urinating. Bed-wetting alarms (found in most pharmacies), however, can alert your child that she is about to wet the bed and can wake her in time to get to the bathroom. The use of these alarms helps your child learn to sense a full bladder on her own. When bed-wetting interferes with normal activity, such as spending the night at a friend's house, you can talk to your pediatrician about possible prescription medications.

**Physical skills your five- and six-year-old needs to master**
Because the life of a five- and six-year-old is so focused on starting school, it's easy to assume that academic skills must take center stage now. But there are underlying physical skills that a healthy child needs to master that support both academic and social well-being. These include fine-motor and large-muscle skills, such as:

*Having independent toilet skills.* Your child should be able to use the school bathroom without help. Barring a physical disability, she should also be adept at controlling her bladder and bowel movements and being able to notify others when she needs to use the toilet.

*Tying, buttoning, zipping, snapping.* The intricacies of bow-tying, especially for tying shoelaces, is a necessary skill by the time your child reaches the end of first grade. By kindergarten, your child should be able to use fasteners on her clothes, to take care of toileting on her own, and to be able to put on her coat with ease.

*Using scissors correctly.* Give your child practice cutting different kinds of paper. Draw outlines of shapes for her to follow. Get your leftie scissors especially designed for left-handed users. Teach her to carry them safely—from the bottom with the blade closed.

*Holding writing, drawing, and eating tools appropriately.* The time for a fist-grasp is over. Help your child learn how to hold tools correctly so she can better manipulate them.

*Kicking, hitting, and catching a ball.* Activities that involve eye-hand (or eye-foot) coordination, such as sports, have a direct correlation to her ability to learn to read and write.

**Balancing.** Standing on one foot without toppling over, walking a balance beam, following the straight-line cracks in the sidewalk—these balancing acts help your child take on many of the social and physical challenges that lie ahead, such as bike riding and gym-class activities. *(For tips on helping your child ride a two-wheeler, see below.)*

**Whistling, snapping fingers, skipping, winking.** While these skills may not have any immediate practical application, they are honored by fives and sixes, and being able to perform them gives your child a certain status among her peers. (So does burping at will, but you probably don't want to encourage that.)

### Tips for riding a two-wheeler

Removing the training wheels, a rite of passage for five- to six-year-olds is also a metaphor for this stage of development. These tips can help make the transition a bit easier:

**Choose the right-size bike.** Don't get a bike that your child will "grow into." From a seated position, the balls of your child's feet should easily touch the ground. If she has to tip-toe to reach the ground, the bike is too big. If, when she's seated, her knees bend and her feet are flat on the ground, the bike's too small.

**Opt for coaster brakes.** For most young kids, bikes with brakes controlled by backpedaling are best, since hand brakes may require more hand strength than your child has yet attained.

**Get to know the bike.** Help your child see what each part of the bike does—the handlebars for steering, the pedals or handbrakes for stopping, the chain to connect the wheels to the gears, and so on.

**Insist on a helmet.** Make donning a helmet a preliminary step to hopping on a bike. Let your child choose a style that suits her and that fits comfortably. Follow the manufacturer's recommendations for fit, and don't allow your child to wear her helmet unlatched or pushed back.

*Choose a safe area.* Practice and riding sessions should be conducted in an area free of car and heavy pedestrian traffic. Also choose a forgiving ground surface such as grass or soft dirt for early practice. On pavement, choose a smooth surface, free of potholes and severe cracks. Make sure whatever area you choose is flat.

*Relax.* Don't make too big a deal out of the experience. Let your child practice getting on and off the bike on her own. Let her become comfortable with the feel of the bike without your hovering.

*Practice balance.* Suggest she try to stay balanced in place with her feet extended. Then, hold the bike steady and let her practice the feel of balancing with her feet on the pedals. Gently guide her forward a few feet so she can feel the forward motion of the pedals. Then let her practice pedaling backward or using the handbrakes to stop. Remind her that as soon as the bike slows to a stop she should extend her feet to maintain balance.

*Start straight, and work up speed.* Make sure her path is clear so that she can concentrate on balance, and not steering, at first. Ask her if she wants to try propelling herself for a length of about 20 feet or so or if she'd rather have you hold on to the seat and run alongside. (Don't hold the handlebars, since doing so will reduce her confidence in her ability to steer.) This step is the nuts and bolts of learning to ride and will probably have to be repeated dozens of times before she's got the knack.

*Practice braking.* Every so often say, "Time to brake," and let your child come to a complete stop and extend her feet to the ground.

*Practice steering.* Set up a simple obstacle course and let her weave or circle around.

*Offer emotional support.* Share stories of your own two-wheeler learning experiences. If she appears to be scared or expresses fear, remind her that learning new things is often scary, but that you have confidence that she'll learn as long as she keeps practicing. Don't ridicule or try to shame her into competence.

*Prepare for mishaps.* Most kids bruise a knee or elbow when learning to ride. Have a first-aid kit close by so that you can attend to a scrape with a minimum of fuss and in a matter-of-fact way.

*Add perseverance to the bike-riding lesson.* If your child wants to give up after a minor fall, consider urging her on. Don't push, however, if she seems overwhelmed. Instead, say something like, "I know you'll be ready to try again soon." If more than a week or so goes by without her asking for more practice time, suggest it yourself.

## YOU AND YOUR CHILD
## How your own judgments about your child affect your relationship

During your child's first year, you no doubt felt a certain amount of anxiety about her development. The second wave of this kind of parental anxiety hits most moms and dads about now, as your child enters school. Will she be able to keep up? Will she excel? Will she make friends? Will her teachers appreciate her unique talents? For the first time, with your child's entry into school, there are other adults, teachers, whose job it is to help raise your child. And once again, some of your sense of self is tied very directly to how well you (and her teachers) perceive your child to be doing.

In your desire to help your child present the best of herself to the world, it can be easy to slip into criticism and to offer unsolicited advice, which your child, once she's reached about five-and-a-half, will perceive as criticism. For example, saying "Why don't you keep your papers neater?" tells your child that she's displeasing you. Accumulating a wealth of papers in her knapsack may represent a very big-kid accomplishment to your new schoolkid. A disparaging remark about them confuses her. "Why can't Mommy be proud of me for having so much school stuff?" she might wonder. A better approach would be to note, "You sure have a lot of papers. I bet there are things in there you'd like me to see." Then, reviewing the papers together, gently demonstrate how to organize them. "Let's put the homework in one pile and keep it in this folder. Let's put the papers you don't need anymore in your desk drawer."

It's all right to admit to yourself if you're worried about a certain aspect of your child's development. It's also a good idea to talk to her pediatrician and her teacher if you have real concerns. Likewise, there may be things about your child's personality that do not sit well with you right now. But it's vital to concentrate on what your child is doing right during this transitional time. Remember: Your role now includes being a safe harbor, the one to return to who loves nonjudgmentally. The emotional support you offer now provides the basis for your child's continued development in both skills and in her sense of self-worth.

## Helping your child appreciate who she is

No matter where your child sees herself in relation to her peers and as a member of your family, work to find ways to celebrate who she is right now. By respecting her individuality, you're letting her know that she's important. Some activities that engender a positive self-awareness are:

*Create a picture collage.* Gather photos and add some art supplies to help your child express how she sees herself. She might, for example, place a picture of herself in the center of a poster board and then glue on magazine cutouts that show things she likes, pictures of her friends and family, or some words that are meaningful to her. Display her collage where everyone can see it.

*Present an award.* Create a trophy or certificate that lets your child know you've noticed a special talent. Even if your child is not a star student, athlete, or musician, help her see that her more subtle talent is every bit as noteworthy. Perhaps she has a remarkable sense of humor. Whatever it is about your child that sets her apart in a positive way, celebrate it.

*Brag.* Let your child overhear you boasting about something she's done. Encourage her to call her grandparents to share with them the story of how she wrote a story in class all by herself.

## HELPING YOUR CHILD GROW
## Fostering resilience

Picture this scenario: Your child comes home from school dejected because she wasn't picked to star in the class play. You might be tempted to say something like, "Well, you're the star to me." If you try to minimize her sense of loss, however, you're missing a chance to help her learn to recover from disappointment. A better approach would be to acknowledge her feelings: "I know you're disappointed. It's hard sometimes not to be picked." As she talks about the event, you can help her gain perspective on it: "There are many opportunities to stand out in school. The play isn't the only one. Maybe you can enter one of your drawings in the art show."

Resilience, the art of bouncing back from disappointment, is, perhaps, the most important skill your child can learn now. In a number of studies, resiliency has been shown to be the deciding factor in achieving success in life. Those born with talents and status can fail to achieve their goals if they are not able to recover from setbacks, while those born with lesser advantages can achieve what they set out to if they've learned to persevere. You can encourage your child's resiliency in a number of ways. For example:

*Give your child opportunities to reverse her losses.* For instance, if she didn't get the grade she'd hoped for on a test, suggest that she ask the teacher to help her find ways to do better next time.

*Help her find a mentor.* Let your child know that you and others are available to help her when she needs it. Knowing that she's not alone to figure out her problems gives your child the confidence to try again.

*Offer her chances to make a difference.* Encourage your child to see herself as a giver as well as a receiver. Let her read to a younger child, have her set the table, encourage her to spend some of her own money to buy a gift for a needy child.

*Assign regular household responsibilities.* Knowing that she's a contributing family member is extremely important to your child—even if she balks at having to do reasonable chores. Be sure to acknowledge her contributions to the running of the household.

*Build on your child's strengths.* Suppose your child is having a hard time learning to read, but happens to be a sports fan who can quote statistics about her favorite player. Help her find books and other materials that relate to her interest. Take her to a ball game and let her buy a souvenir program, then help her read the picture captions as a first step to reading the whole program.

*Believe in your child.* The most important factor in raising a child who believes in herself is having a loving adult believe in her. When you let your child know that you love her, trust her, and have hopes for her, she can enjoy high self-esteem and the knowledge that she is capable of facing and overcoming whatever comes her way.

# Ready or not, here I come!

## Your child's school readiness

Sending your child off to kindergarten or first grade can conjure up the same mixture of excitement and anxiety you felt when he was a toddler first venturing into the sandbox. And just as those early playground experiences evolved from unnerving to enjoyable, so too can your child's entry into formal schooling grow from a worry-tinged foray into the unknown to a pleasant everyday routine.

The regularity with which kids and their parents adapt and adjust to the routine of formal schooling, however, does not detract from the importance of the adventure. Starting kindergarten or first grade is, after all, a major step toward maturity, and it requires preparation. The good news is that there are simple things you can do to help your child get off to the right start at school. This chapter explains what you need to know about kindergarten and making the transition to first grade.

**DEVELOPMENTAL MILESTONE**
## School readiness

As the parent of a five-year-old, your first question is probably: Is my child ready for school? So much about early-childhood, preschool, and early-grade-school education has been in flux for the last few decades that parents and educators both are unsure of just what constitutes school readiness. There is a consensus on one thing, however: School readiness is a two-way street. Children have to be ready with some basic skills. And schools have to be ready to meet the needs of a range of students. A child may be ready for a full-day kindergarten that stresses social skills and learning through play. But he may not be ready for a program that focuses on academic skills. Readiness, then, amounts to a good match between a particular child and a particular classroom.

To know if your child is ready for the school to which you plan to enroll him, you need to look at both your child and the school. If your child has been attending a nursery school, his teacher is a great source of information about how his maturity and skill level compares to that of other kindergarten-bound kids. She has not only observed your child in a classroom setting, but she has had the opportunity to observe dozens and perhaps hundreds of kids his age, giving her a more objective viewpoint than your own about his readiness. A look at the kindergarten of your choice can fill you in on teacher expectations as well as the school's curriculum. And a peek inside the classroom tells you if the class is made up primarily of five- or six-year-olds. The age level of your child's potential classmates should, in most cases, match your child's age.

**The emotional and social skills your kindergartner needs**
School readiness is often thought to include a list of academic achievements. Primarily, however, readiness for kindergarten, especially those designed for five-year-olds, hinges on emotional maturity. Signs of emotional readiness include:

*The ability to communicate his needs and wants verbally.* Your child should have the confidence and the vocabulary to address a teacher and fellow classmates.

*The ability to compromise and negotiate with his peers.* A kindergartner needs to be aware of other people's opinions and desires and be able to incorporate them into his own decision-making process.

*An acceptance of teachers' and administrators' authority.* Kindergartners need to know that you support teachers and other adults in the school and that he, too, is expected to abide by the school rules.

*The independence to work alone and with groups.* Your child should be able to separate from you and work independently or with his peers without constant adult intervention.

*A degree of focus.* A kindergartner should be able to remain "on task"—he should be able to see a project through from beginning to end without undue adult intervention.

*A curiosity about the world.* Being an eager explorer and enthusiastic learner underlies a kindergartner's readiness for school.

## The academic skills your kindergartner needs

No school expects five-year-olds to arrive at kindergarten already reading and doing complex math. However, there are some basic skills that your child should have mastered by the time he enters kindergarten:

*Identifying colors.* Your child should be able to name four or five basic colors, such as black, white, green, red, blue, or yellow.

*Naming basic shapes.* Your child should be able to recognize, name, and draw a circle, a square, and perhaps a triangle.

*Knowing most letters.* The alphabet song should be familiar to your five-year-old. Upon entering kindergarten, most kids recognize the letters in their names (or at least the initial letter) as well as a few others. Some can recognize all or most uppercase letters of the alphabet, and a few know lowercase letters as well.

*Understanding that letters makes sounds and that putting letters together makes words.* Your child need not know all the letter sounds on the first day of school, of course. But he should be aware that each letter has its own sound or sounds and that letters make words.

*Knowing how books "work."* By age five, your child should know that books contain stories and other writing, should know that words tell the story, and should be aware that reading is done from the top of the page to the bottom and from left to right.

*Knowing the numbers one through ten.* Most kids can recognize most of the written numerals from 1 to 10 and know that each numeral corresponds to a certain number of items. Some can do simple addition and subtraction.

*Understanding space and size relationship words.* Your child should be familiar with the meanings of words such as *over/under, big/small, near/far,* and *back/front.*

## Preparing your child for kindergarten

There's no need to buy flashcards to prepare your child for kindergarten. The learning that he's done at home and in a preschool program, if he's attended one, are all the preparation he really needs. It's been said, however, that formal schooling is really just an extension of home schooling, because, especially in the early grades, you remain your child's primary teacher. The home schooling that serves your child as a prelude to kindergarten and beyond includes the following:

*Help your child develop a strong relationship with books.* Read to your child every day. This is the most important step you can take to prepare him for school. Don't reserve reading just for bedtime, either. Read during the day, when he is more alert. Encourage your child to choose books, to handle them, and to "read" to you, whether he makes up a story based on the pictures he sees or whether he's reciting an oft-read story from memory.

*Talk to your child about everyday tasks.* Count with him as you set the table, show him how you measure ingredients when cooking, let him help you sort the laundry by color and match socks by size.

*Give him lots of opportunities to play with other children.* Your child needs to practice cooperating and negotiating with his peers as well as having opportunities to learn from them.

*Encourage the use of language.* Ask your child's opinion about events. Prompt him to use words to express his feelings and to tell you what's on his mind. Let him tell you about a project he's doing.

**The ability to comply with teachers' expectations**

Making the transition from a little kid to a kindergartner fills your child with a range of emotions. He's proud of joining the big-kid world. He's excited, and maybe a little nervous, about meeting the demands of the classroom. He's also a bit torn about his feelings for the teacher. If the teacher is a woman, he may feel somewhat guilty about any affection he feels for her, equating his new love for his teacher as a disloyalty to Mom. (This is true for girls as well as boys.) If the teacher has corrected him or simply not responded to him immediately when he wanted attention, he may be furious and feel that the teacher doesn't like him. His need to be liked by the teacher is overwhelming and any perceived slight is taken to heart.

Surprisingly, as grown up as he now is, he may not associate his classroom behavior with his teacher's response to him. A child who wants the teacher's attention, for instance, may whine for it, only to be told to wait. He may "tattle," telling the teacher, for instance, that another child is not sitting down when he should be. His motivation may be to call the teacher's attention to the fact that he himself *is* sitting. He may be surprised when he's not congratulated for pointing out the other child's behavior.

As the year continues and as your child matures further, he will develop a new relationship with his teacher, based on his experiences both in and out of the classroom. If you demonstrate that you support the learning process and the teacher, your child will most likely come to share your view that classroom cooperation and responsibility for carrying out school assignments are important, and he will strive to abide by the teacher's authority. If, however, you indicate any disrespect for the teacher or the school or otherwise undermine the teacher's place in your child's life, he'll have a harder time finding his place in the classroom.

For most children, the support of both their parents and teachers combines to help them work out their relationship with their teacher. By five-and-a-half, in fact, the teacher may temporarily supplant you as your child's favorite person. He'll begin sentences with "My teacher says . . ." as a way of letting you know that you no longer know everything. The change from a preschooler to a school kid will begin to feel natural to both of you. He'll develop a swagger, and this confident gait will let you know that he has, indeed, with your and his teacher's help, made a successful leap in maturity.

## What to look for in a kindergarten setting

As you look at options, these are the things, in general, that promote a good kindergarten experience to which you should be alert:

*Appropriate class size.* Fewer than 25 but more than 12 children should be the rule. In larger classes, kids can't get the teacher's attention and may not receive intervention—such as an answer to a question—when they need it. Between 14 and 20 students is optimal for grades K through 2. This class size allows one-on-one time between the teacher and each student as well as providing for a good range of skill levels and personalities within a class. Too-small classes, fewer than 10 students especially, can also be problematic. In very small classes, kids can feel overly scrutinized and "on" all the time. This can lead some to performance anxiety and fear of making mistakes. And since boys and girls tend to separate socially at this age, five or fewer potential playmates in a class can create social problems, leading some kids to feel excluded and unable to find a friend whose play style and interests match their own. Special-education classes, however, do tend to be smaller, which is appropriate for children with special needs.

*A dedicated, professional teaching staff.* A kindergarten teacher is not a glorified baby-sitter. He or she needs a strong background in early-childhood education, an ability to respond in a caring way to the emotional and academic needs of a number of kids, a high degree of patience, and the stamina to energize, and channel the energy of, more than a dozen young children. He or she organizes the students by gaining cooperation respectfully rather than by intimidation. The teacher also should be a good communicator with both children and parents and actively seek to bring each parent into the learning process.

*A clean and safe physical space.* The school building, grounds, and individual classrooms should have good lighting, clean air, and an overall inviting appearance. Each early-grade classroom should also have areas dedicated to special activities, such as a building corner and a reading area. There should be enough room between children, and between desks and other equipment, so that kids and adults can move freely and safely around the room.

*A dedicated, professional administration.* The school administrator in a well-run school works closely with her teachers to assure that each has the support needed for classroom success. The administrator needs to be a good communicator to ensure that the school, teachers, children, and parents are all aware of and working toward the same goals. A good administrator has a vision for the school and is able to share that vision clearly and gain the support of others in the educational community.

### The kindergarten curriculum

The best curriculum for your child is the one that best matches his learning style. A learning agenda and teaching method, for instance, in which children spend a lot of time at their desks and work mostly in large groups, may be just right for some children. That same classroom would be wrong for a child who needs to be more active and more independent or who needs more one-on-one time with the teacher. Ideally, you will be able to choose the best program. However, if your only option is the local school that may not be "perfect," don't assume that your child will be traumatized.

With your support, your child will most likely adapt and even thrive in an environment that offers some, but not all, of what you'd hoped for. After-school activities can augment classroom experiences. Lots of down time at home where your child can run around or laze about can counter an overactive or underactive classroom. Remember: Your five-year-old wants to please, wants to be part of the group. Most likely, he'll rise to the challenge and adjust quite well to the classroom he's in. There are, however, certain elements that all good kindergartens share:

*Respect for each individual child.* A good kindergarten is flexible enough to allow for different styles and rates of learning. There are activities for children who have already mastered the basic curriculum as well as for those who need extra help and practice. Children's personal cultures and individual histories are woven into the context of learning.

*They engender a love of learning.* Children's curiosity is inspired and their problem-solving skills honed in ways that allow for different approaches from different learners. A good kindergarten energizes rather than tires children.

*A celebration of reading.* Books and other reading materials are readily available. Teachers read throughout the day, not just during "storytime," helping kids to value and enjoy the magic of books.

*Lots of time for creative and physical play.* Children have many opportunities to create artwork, act out a play, and let off steam at recess and other times.

*Skills are taught in an integrated way.* A good kindergarten involves children's play in learning. For example, children might learn math concepts by setting a table for a picnic, learning to count out plates and cups. Cooking and building activities are used to help kids understand language, science, and math concepts.

**The classroom is an active, social place.** Children work together in small groups as well as individually and in whole-class groupings.

**A *variety of play and learning equipment.*** Space and time are devoted to books, blocks, dress-up play, art, and music.

**The classroom decor celebrates students.** The classroom is decorated with children's artwork and written stories, complete with made-up spelling, typically using consonants, but very few vowels (*k-t* for cat, for example).

**Students are exposed to authentic art, literature, and music.** Through visiting artists and field trips as well as classroom activities, children experience and learn to appreciate the broader culture.

### The academic skills kindergarten teachers teach

In addition to the many social skills they learn by being valued members of the class, kindergartners generally learn the following academic skills in a classroom designed for fives:

**Letter names and sounds.** By the end of the school year, most children will have learned to recognize uppercase letters, to name them, and to know what sound(s) each letter makes. Many children will also know how to recognize lowercase letters.

**Prereading or reading.** Children in kindergarten begin to learn to decode words phonetically and to recognize frequently seen words, such as *the* and *of* by sight. Most importantly, they learn to value reading and to enjoy listening to stories being read as well as discovering some books on their own.

**Writing.** Kindergartners learn to express themselves on paper, using a combination of letter shapes, pictures, and invented spelling to tell a story.

*Math concepts.* Children learn such concepts as more and less and bigger and smaller. They learn to recognize numerals and to count, at least through ten and possibly up to 100 or beyond. They will learn one-to-one correspondence, such as learning that ten stuffed animals need ten plates for their picnic. They will learn to recognize patterns and to create patterns, such as making a row of five red marks, two blue, five red, two yellow, and so on.

*Life sciences.* Children will observe and discuss the life of plants and class pets and learn the basics of hygiene and good nutrition.

In classrooms designed for sixes, the following are usually added to the curriculum:

*Reading.* Children are focused on reading age-appropriate materials, choosing books, and retelling stories in their own words.

*Simple math.* Children are taught simple addition and, possibly, subtraction.

## What your kindergartner's day might be like
A half-day program will include a mix of meeting time, small-group lessons, whole-group activities, and breaks for snacks and outdoor play. A full-day program will likely include these elements:

*Morning meeting.* Attendance is taken; children and teacher discuss what day of the week it is; special events, such as a child's birthday, are noted; the weather is recorded; students recite the Pledge of Allegiance; jobs are posted, such as which child will help distribute the day's snack; and any homework is collected.

*Small-group play and learning time.* Groups of children work on various projects, from artwork to alphabet recognition. These group times usually occur both in the morning and in the afternoon.

*Group experience.* The whole class gathers for a whole-group activity like a storytelling session or a lesson about the classroom rabbit. There are usually two such whole-group activities per day.

*Lunch.*

*Recess.* Either after lunch or both in the morning and afternoon, preferably outdoors.

*Rest time.* Many kindergarten classrooms include quiet time or naptime in the afternoon.

*Special class.* Many kindergarten curricula include a special class each day, such as art, music, gym, or science, for which the whole class goes to another place within the school.

*End-of-day time.* Any homework assignments are given and notes to take home are distributed. (Don't forget to check that backpack!) Children gather their things before leaving for home or the school's after-school program.

## The right age for kindergarten

In the 1990s, researchers began to look seriously at the phenomenon of delayed kindergarten admission. Some educators have concluded that kids born late in the year do benefit from what many call "the gift of time" in delaying school entry, especially when kindergarten includes a host of academic work. The vast majority, however, backed by long-term research, conclude that the shift to late starting can do far more harm than good, especially when it results in a child being a year older than his classmates. And in cases in which all the kids begin school later, the researchers note that this only serves to exacerbate the problem of pushing academic learning downward into kindergarten, since it encourages schools to redesign the kindergarten curriculum for six-year-olds.

## Testing for school admission

There's absolutely no need to have your child tested if the school of your choice does not require it and if you or his preschool teacher believe that he has no learning disabilities. If the school of your choice requires testing or if you feel that testing would help you evaluate your child's school readiness, be sure to find a tester who has experience working with young children. Your child's pediatrician or the school or state university should be able to refer you to a competent tester. Be sure, too, that the test being used is a valid measurement tool for what you need to know. (Call your state university's education department and ask if the test being administered is appropriate. Some, such as the Stanford-Binet, are used for assessment. There are a host of different diagnostic tests to detect various learning disorders.)

Also realize that young children are notoriously unpredictable test takers. If you think your child's test results are not in keeping with your own evaluation, have him retested so that you can compare the results. As far as preparation, cramming will do no good. Instead, for assessment tests, the best preparation includes a regular routine of reading to your child, allowing him the time and the tools to express himself artistically, and exposing him to mathematical concepts. On the day of the test, make sure your child is well-rested and not hungry. Impart the importance of doing his best, but don't share any anxiety you may be feeling with him.

The National Association for the Education of Young Children (NAEYC) has taken the lead in resisting (and in many cases over-turning) the shift to late kindergarten admission, stressing that chronological age should be the prime factor in determining when a child begins kindergarten. The NAEYC also favors a kindergarten curriculum that includes lots of play along with a gentle introduction to academics, a curriculum that best supports the learning style of most five-year-olds.

Educators and child-development experts largely concur that a child who has enjoyed a good preschool program is ready at the age of five or nearly five for an appropriate kindergarten curriculum.

And, the NAEYC notes, those who seem to be lagging could find no better place to catch up to their peers than in a classroom full of their peers. Moreover, if a child has a learning disability, especially one that is not readily apparent, delaying school-based assessment and treatment could place a child even further behind his peers when he does finally start school.

Researchers whose work supports kindergarten admission at age five concede that some younger children may, in fact, struggle a bit more in the early school years. But, they observe that by grade three, the differences in achievement between those who begin kindergarten at age five and those who begin at age six disappear, and, in many cases, the younger children outperform the older ones. Moreover, the late-starting kids, especially if they are older than their classmates, begin to show more behavioral and academic problems from adolescence onward than do their younger classmates.

### What if you disagree with the school on the right starting age?
If you feel your child is chronologically and otherwise ready to begin school but the school of your choice disagrees, consider your options. Learn about all the schools in your area that your child may be eligible to attend. Can you enroll your child in a different district or in another school within the district, either public, private, or parochial, that has a different starting age or is more flexible in its admission policy? Does the school you wish your child to attend have a pre-K program from which your child could proceed with his peers to first grade, skipping kindergarten? Are there other parents who share your views about an earlier admission date with whom you could join to lobby the school or the district about reevaluating their policy?

If you feel your child really should start kindergarten older than his classmates, be aware that the school might surprise you next year at enrollment time and insist that he go directly to first grade, thereby missing the kindergarten experience entirely. Investigate your school's policies for admission so you're not caught off guard.

There's one more thing to remember if you plan to send your child to school where the starting age is later or earlier than you think it should be: If you expect him to attend school there through grade school and move on to high school with many of the same kids, then a later or earlier starting age may not be a problem. The important thing is that your child not be significantly out of sync, age-wise, with his classmates.

*Should kindergarten admission ever be delayed?* There are some cases in which a child could benefit from a delay in school entry:

♦ **Very low birth weight or prematurity.** If your child was born under three pounds or at less than eight months gestation, you may want to consider his adjusted age rather than his birth date in determining readiness.

♦ **The age of classmates.** If your five-year-old seems ready and eager for kindergarten but would be entering a class of children who are significantly older (averaging a year or more older) consider enrolling him in an appropriate pre-K program before kindergarten. Or, if you have the option, enroll him in another school in which his age is more average for the kindergarten classroom.

If your child has a developmental lag, be aware that enrolling him in kindergarten may be required to ensure that he receives appropriate intervention to which he is entitled by law.

*When should you make the decision about starting school?* In most schools, enrollment takes place during the spring before your child will begin school. It's essential that you stay abreast of the requirements for the school you're interested in. Some popular magnet schools, elite private schools, and overcrowded neighborhood schools can deny admission if you don't apply very early, sometimes as far in advance as the autumn or winter of the year prior to admission. Also, registering at the last minute can be a somewhat chaotic experience as school administrators need to shuffle class lists to accommodate unexpected students.

## Record keeping: Papers to have on hand for school registration

In order to register your child for school, you'll need to have some paperwork in order. At least a month or so before you plan to register, call the school or district to find out exactly what you'll need to bring with you. Also be aware that some schools require that your child be present at registration while others allow you to register without him there.

The papers you're likely to need include:
- **Record of age.** You'll need a birth or baptismal certificate or other proof of age.
- **Records from preschool.** If your child has attended preschool, you may need to bring a teacher's report along.
- **Medical forms.** You'll need proof that your child has received all required immunizations, or proof that you have received a waiver for religious or other reasons.
- **Medical records.** If your child qualifies for special services because of a physical, emotional, or mental disability, have certification of his condition available to ensure that your child receives the services to which he's entitled at the start of the school year.
- **Proof of citizenship or legal residency.** In some states and districts you'll need to show proof of your child's citizenship or legal residency. In most, however, this is not required.
- **Proof of address.** You'll need to show a current phone or electric bill, mortgage statement, or lease to prove that you reside in the area served by the school if your child is to attend a local public school that is not a charter school.
- **Financial records.** If you qualify for free school lunch, many districts will want to see proof of your income. The same is true if you plan to apply for financial aid from private or parochial schools.

If you're concerned about whether your child will be ready at the start of the school year, it's best to assume that he will, and proceed with the admission process on schedule. Many kids who seem to be lagging may be caught up by the time school begins. Don't forestall making the decision too long, however, since your child needs a bit of time to get used to the idea of being a kindergartner. Ideally, by June of the year in which he'll start (if starting time is September), you'll know if and where he'll be attending kindergarten.

## CONFLICT
## Frustration with the demands and pace of learning

Within days or weeks of the excitement of starting school, your child will no doubt be hit with a remarkable insight: School is an ongoing thing. Beyond the new book bag and the sharpened pencils, there is a day-to-dayness of the experience that he wasn't prepared for. He may decide sometime in October that he's had enough of school. "It's boring," he might protest. Or, "It's too hard."

He may be angry at the teacher for asking him to do work he doesn't feel like doing or doesn't feel capable of doing. With his teacher, he's not so sure how to get out of doing what's expected of him if the mood doesn't strike him or if he's unsure of how to proceed. So, in the classroom, he may plow ahead and then fall to pieces at home with you because he has to let his feelings out somewhere.

While most kindergartners find some things about school less than perfect, they generally love being in school. When he feels overchallenged or underchallenged, however, problems can occur. If your child feels bored by certain aspects of the classroom experience, it's important to talk with his teacher about finding ways to challenge him appropriately. This may include after-school activities at home and in settings such as a pee-wee soccer team or an after-school reading club. If your child is struggling with some parts of the school day, meet with the teacher to work out a plan that will boost both your child's tenacity and his skill level. Be sure to reassure your child that you have confidence in his ability to do the work, and offer practical support—such as extra reading time at home or after-school playtime that incorporates the skills he needs to learn. Playing cards, for instance, can help him become more familiar with numbers. Be sure that you don't become overbearing about repeating the work he's doing at school that's frustrating him. At home, he may need relief from the pressures he's feeling, not more pressure to perform. Remind your child that it's his job to learn, but assure him that you don't expect him to learn everything all at once.

## Easing your child's fear of starting school

Transitions are difficult for many children. Ironically, kids who thrive best on a predictable schedule may have the hardest time adjusting to the new routine of school, at least at the onset of the school year before the school schedule becomes old hat. For most kids, it's the fear of the unknown that triggers concerns. To help your child feel more at ease with the new experience, try these activities a few weeks before the start of school:

*Offer a preview.* Take your child to visit the school he'll be attending before classes start. If possible, introduce him to his teacher. Let him know where the important rooms are—his classroom, the office, the auditorium, and, most important, the school bathroom. (Kindergartners often have their own, separate from the older children's bathrooms.) Ask an upbeat current kindergartner to explain to your child what your child's day will be like. Try to meet and set up a playdate with a child who will be your child's classmate. If your child will be riding a school bus, try to arrange a school bus tour, too.

*Read school-based storybooks.* Ask the children's librarian or local bookstore for suggestions on books that discuss the start-of-school experience.

*Buy cool supplies.* Let your child pick out a backpack, pencils, and other supplies that reflect his new status as a schoolkid.

*Incorporate some "school" activities to your home routine.* For example, introduce afternoon storytime or snack time.

*Share your own positive memories of your start of school.* Your child will love hearing that you, too, once experienced the same feelings and events that he's now going through.

A few days before school begins:

*Help your child pick out an appropriate first-day outfit.* Have him try it on to make sure there's nothing itchy or otherwise uncomfortable about it.

*Adjust his schedule ahead of time.* If the start of kindergarten signals a change in your child's schedule, ease into the new schedule beforehand, including an earlier bedtime and earlier rising so that he won't be exhausted by a sudden shift of his internal clock.

On the first day:

*Get up early.* Enjoy a favorite breakfast together at a leisurely pace.

*Take your child to school or to the bus stop a little early.* Don't go so early that the wait will trigger worry, though.

*Accompany your child if possible.* Escort your child into his classroom, help him find his desk and cubby, and help him introduce himself to his teacher and classmates.

*Keep your good-byes brief.* Reassure your child that you will be there as soon as school is over. Remind him to have a good time.

| If your child . . . | Do say | Don't say |
|---|---|---|
| clings to you as you drop him off at school | "I trust you to have a good day. I look forward to hearing all about it." | "There's nothing to be afraid of. Don't be such a baby." |
| says, "My teacher doesn't like me" | "Let's figure out ways for you to get to know each other better so you can find things about each other to like." | "I'm sure she likes you," or "Maybe she'd like you better if you were neater." |
| says, "I'll never learn to write my name" | "Lots of kids feel that way at first. Let's work on it together." Then remind your child of all the things he has learned with practice. | "Sure you will," or "You just have to work harder." |

## YOU AND YOUR CHILD
# Supporting your child's learning

While starting your child in kindergarten represents your commitment to sharing the responsibility for his education with his teacher, it should not involve any withdrawal from your own role as his teacher nor any form of competition with his teacher. How can you best be supportive of his teacher?

Know the teacher's expectations. Attend any meetings that outline the curriculum for parents. Read all notes that the teacher sends home. Take a moment before or after school at the start of the school year to meet with the teacher to discuss any questions or concerns you might have.

***Read to your child.*** Some children resist learning to read when they sense that independent reading means they'll lose out on your reading to them. Continue to read to your child daily in a relaxed manner. Don't interrupt your reading with quizzes such as "Find the word *apple* in the story," unless your child indicates that he wants to demonstrate what he's learning. Other children simply aren't ready to learn to read at five. Don't push it. Many, many children do not read fluently until first or second grade.

*Continue to enjoy math and science encounters.* Enlist your child to help you measure ingredients for a recipe or count out stamps to match the number of envelopes you're mailing. As with reading, however, don't make every activity one in which your child needs to perform for you.

*Encourage your child's language skills.* Take a trip to the zoo on weekends so that your child has something interesting to report during class meetings and in his writing. Many children, when asked to "write" about a topic of their choosing, are at a loss to think of something interesting to talk about. After a zoo adventure, mention that seeing the monkeys swing from the vines would be a fun thing to share with his classmates and teacher.

*Offer practical support.* If your child seems confused by any aspects of learning, work with him in a nonjudgmental manner to help him gain the skills he needs.

*Assure lots of play time.* School is only one aspect of your child's life. Make sure he has the time to enjoy other pursuits.

*Reduce other stresses.* By its very nature, school is challenging. Working to meet those challenges can cause your child stress. Signs of school stress include extreme fatigue, excess grouchiness, acute sensitivity to any criticism, and a lessening of interest in things he usually enjoys. To keep stress from becoming a regular part of your child's school experience, make a special point of limiting additional causes for anxiety. Plan fun family activities. Give your kindergartner some space, if he needs it, from siblings. Don't expose your child to any potentially scary movies. Be a good listener.

## Developing a partnership with your child's teacher

The alliance you form with your child's teacher will go a long way toward promoting your child's school success, both this year and in the future. To forge a positive working relationship with your child's teacher:

*Open the lines of communication early.* Early in the school year, meet with or write to your child's teacher to help her get to know your child better. Tell the teacher about your child's interests and personality. Share any details about your child's home life that could help the teacher better understand him, such as the birth of a new sibling, an illness in the family, a divorce or separation, or another event that may affect your child's concentration.

*Attend all meetings.* Teachers and administrators set aside time each year to address parents' concerns. Make use of this time, if at all possible, rather than asking for separate explanations of things that are divulged at PTA meetings or other functions.

*Volunteer.* In addition to making yourself available to chaperone class trips, volunteer inside the classroom, too. It will give you insight into your child's day as well as signaling to the teacher that you're there to support her efforts.

*Address concerns as they arise.* Don't wait until the more hurried scheduled meeting between teachers and parents to communicate any problems. Addressed early, you can prevent small problems from becoming larger ones. When you ask for a private conference, make sure you tell the teacher the topic you'd like to discuss to give her a chance to prepare to respond to your concerns.

*Be prepared at parent-teacher conferences.* Make a list of questions beforehand so that you can use your allotted time to your and the teacher's best advantage.

*Share any positive feelings you have.* Thank the teacher either in person or with a brief note when your child has benefited from her instruction.

*Address any negative thoughts in a nonjudgmental way.* Be as specific as possible. Rather than saying, "My child is unhappy at school and I want to know what's wrong," rephrase your comment as something like, "He's having trouble with math, especially telling sixes and nines apart. What do you suggest we do to help him?"

## Handling homework

Even in kindergartens that are not focused on academic subjects, there can be homework—anything from remembering to bring in old baby pictures, to collecting fallen leaves, to practicing writing a page of *A*'s. The kindergarten year is the best time to establish good attitudes and homework rituals that work for your child. For starters:

*Set aside a special time for homework.* Some kids work best right after school, while others prefer to play, snack, and just hang out before focusing on homework. Find the time that suits your child's energy level, mood, and that works best in the family's schedule. As much as possible, dedicate this time to homework every evening so that homework becomes a part of the routine.

*Designate a special place to work.* Your child might prefer to work at the kitchen table while you prepare dinner or may find it easier to tackle homework at his own desk, away from the noise of the household. Let your child choose the place that works best for him. One caveat: Make sure that his homework won't be interrupted midway by family members.

***Help your child develop a can-do attitude.*** Let your child know that homework is his job. However, don't let him struggle through it alone. Make sure that he has the materials he needs, that he understands the assignment, and that he knows he can turn to you for guidance when he's not sure of what to do.

***Communicate with the teacher.*** As with all other matters concerning your child's school day, let the teacher know if any particular homework is proving difficult for your child.

## Making the transition to first grade

Even after a successful kindergarten year, the transition to first grade is a big step for your child. The focus shifts from an introductory phase to a different kind of productive stage. In first grade, there may be less classroom playtime and more time in which children devote themselves to learning specific things, especially reading.

A good curriculum continues to take six-year-olds' development into account. Learning is still largely based on handling real objects, not just sitting and listening. Social skills continue to be honed. The introduction of more formal classroom experiences is likely, including worksheets that involve your child in problem-solving practice.

# What I know and how I learn

## Your child's learning style

As a new five-year-old, your child is still at the concrete stage of learning, whereby handling objects gives her an understanding of the world. By five-and-a-half, she's making a monumental leap into the world of ideas. Abstract concepts such as time and feelings begin to make sense to her. The manner in which she learns goes through a transformation, too, as she moves from learning primarily through direct observation to learning through language, logic, and other means.

"Smart" used to mean just two things: how well a child used and understood language and how well she understood logical and mathematical concepts. While language and math skills continue to dominate the school curricula, educators now know that children acquire knowledge and best demonstrate what they know in a variety of ways. No longer is a child's intelligence seen to be based solely on how well she can repeat what she hears and sees in the classroom. Increasingly, other abilities—to socialize well; to be adept at music, art, or sports; her level of self-awareness, her awareness of others—have come to be understood as aspects of her intelligence. Along with the recognition that children can be smart in a number of different ways came the realization that different children have distinct learning styles.

The way your child most naturally behaves is your best clue to her personal learning style. If your child is very active and loves to dance, her most comfortable style of learning probably involves movement. If your child is quiet and somewhat serious, her natural learning style will most likely involve some introspection.

Researchers have identified seven common ways in which children acquire knowledge. By being alert to your child's learning style, you can be in a better position to help her learn as well as provide the best opportunities for her to demonstrate what she knows. Following are the seven kinds of intelligence and examples of how each learning style might show itself in a typical kindergarten or first-grade lesson on how a seed becomes a plant:

***Word smart: linguistic learner.*** A word-smart learner learns by listening, reading, speaking, and writing. If your child is word smart, reading or hearing the teacher talk about seeds and preparing a written or an oral report helps her both grasp the material and demonstrate her understanding of it.

***Logic smart: logical-mathematical learner.*** A logic-smart child learns by observing and experimenting with number and science concepts. If a teacher posed a "what if" question such as "What would happen if the seed didn't get any water?" your logic-smart learner's understanding of the material would be heightened. She would also learn by conducting her own experiments.

*Picture smart: spatial learner.* The picture-smart child sees what casual observers miss. She can visualize easily and can use mental images to create drawings and structures. If your child is picture smart, she learns best by reviewing images (actual, and in photos and drawings) and can best demonstrate her understanding with drawings or by creating 3-D images such as dioramas showing how the seed is planted in the soil and the plant grows up from the roots.

*Music smart: musical learner.* If your child is music smart, she best grasps information that's presented melodically. She easily retains ideas contained in songs and jingles as well as in rhythmic poetry. Her learning is also enhanced simply by having music playing in the background while she works on a project or observes a lesson. A song or poem about seeds or plants would help her understand the lesson. (Learning the alphabet through reciting the alphabet song is a perfect learning activity for a music-smart child.)

*Body smart: bodily-kinesthetic learner.* A body-smart child learns in physical ways, through her senses and through movement. Most young children have a predisposition to body learning. If your child is body-smart, she may come to understand the life of a seed by handling one, cutting it apart to see how it feels, and perhaps by tasting it, too. A body-smart child learns best when she's allowed to move around while she's learning. A romp through a garden and class time spent digging and planting would be just right for her.

*People smart: interpersonal.* If your child is people smart, she learns best as part of a group—working with others, listening to different viewpoints, and expressing her own opinion. Engaging in a talk about how seeds become plants, even arguing about it, can help her understand the lesson and show what she knows.

*Self-smart: intrapersonal.* Your self-smart child learns through introspection. In learning about plants, she thinks about how plants make her feel, and might even consider how a seed or plant itself feels. She might want to dress up as a plant and talk about what her life is like as a way of showing her knowledge. As she gets older and more adept at writing, your self-smart child will probably enjoy keeping a diary to record her thoughts and feelings.

While all children learn through a combination of styles, every child also has a natural inclination toward just one or two styles at different stages in her development. At five, your child probably learns best in a body-smart way. At five-and-a-half, her approach may move more toward musical learning, and by six-and-a-half be oriented more toward learning through language. Different strengths emerge as they are needed or as a result of the child's experience.

## DEVELOPMENTAL MILESTONE
# Abstract thinking

When your child first learned to identify animals, she may have concluded that all four-legged creatures were dogs. Being able to differentiate four-legged animals from two-legged humans was a big step for her. Now, she can distinguish dogs from cats from rhinos from cows quite readily. She's even able to narrow her classifications into smaller and smaller categories, identifying a dog as a Dalmation, for example, and even further as a female Dalmatian puppy. This delineation, while a major step in cognition, still represents a concrete understanding of the world. For your five-year-old, categories remain confused and kids tend to make overgeneralizations. For example, your child's limited understanding of the world may still lead her to conclude that all mommies like jogging and all daddies like tennis because that's how it is in your family. Similarly, if your child has ever been frightened by a dog, she may conclude that all dogs are scary. An accumulation of experiences will help her sort out her understanding, as will your gently pointing out inconsistencies in her logic. Saying, for instance, "It's true that I like to jog and daddy likes tennis. But Jeremy's mom plays tennis, and Bianca's dad likes to jog" helps your child reorganize her thinking. By six or six-and-a-half, your child's understanding is far more complex and allows for exceptions to the rules of life she's understood thus far. She'll know, for instance, that another person can have a vastly different opinion on a subject than she has. She'll even be able to weigh that opinion against her own and come to a new conclusion if the evidence conflicts with her prior understanding.

By the time your child is ready for kindergarten, she has also acquired a limited understanding of abstract concepts. She firmly knows, for instance, the difference between now and later, and even yesterday and tomorrow. Until about the age of five-and-a-half, she curtails any misbehaviors simply because she wants to please you. Your "do this" and "don't do that" set the parameters for her actions. As she moves toward six, however, and increasingly as she approaches age seven, she begins to develop an understanding of right and wrong that is not always tied to your directives.

Your child's learning style is also affected by her entry into the world of abstract thinking. She will progress to learning through listening or by concentrating on her feelings, rather than just by handling objects. Until around age seven, she will still believe in magic and the power of wishes, but her feet are becoming more firmly planted in the real world. Throughout these years, she's gaining a firmer grasp of what is and what isn't true. She's ready to interpret the world in a new way. She goes from knowing that a certain magnetic letter on the refrigerator is a thing called a "B" to understanding that the shape "B" is a symbol that stands for a sound that is combined with other symbols and sounds to form words. This movement from the concrete to the abstract underlies your child's ability to learn to read and to work with mathematical concepts as well as to become more adept at social skills, sports, music, and visual arts.

## How your child learns math concepts

Your child has already learned the basic language of math, such as more and less or some and none. She also knows that numerals represent the idea of quantity. At home, you can incorporate math concepts into your child's life as a continuation of her normal play and as an extension of the math instruction she's receiving at school, which is typically oriented around problem solving. During play, work in activities that mimic those likely to be found in her classroom.

For example, in a typical kindergarten or first-grade class, your child might be presented with ten blocks and this problem: How many ways can you arrange these ten blocks into two groups? Working with classmates together in groups of three or four, the children might divide the blocks into two sets of five. Then they might go on to make one set of four and one of six. Some may approach the problem very systematically until the ten blocks are put into all possible configurations of two.

From there, the teacher may help the children discover that "3 + 7" blocks is the same as "7 + 3" blocks. During the lesson, children learn to say the problem in their own words, to figure out what information they need to solve the problem, to experiment with different ways of solving it, and to decide if their answers make sense.

Besides calculations, such as adding 2 and 2 or subtracting 4 from 5, children in the primary grades learn the concepts that underlie these calculations. For example, your child will learn about:

***Patterns and relationships.*** This involves learning that numbers can tell the order of events—first, second, and last; that in the pattern 1, 2, . . ., 4, the 3 is missing; that shapes can be classified according to size (small, smaller, and smallest) or by the number of sides (three on a triangle, and four on a rectangle). They learn that the day in school follows a certain predictable schedule: first reading, then lunch, then recess, then home.

**Number concepts.** Number concepts include knowing that the numeral 5 stands for five objects and that in the numeral 52 the 5 stands for 50. It also includes knowing that 7 is more than 6 but less than 8.

**Estimation.** Through estimation, children learn to use visual clues to make a reasonable guess. For example, they might see a cup full of jelly beans and learn to guess that there may be about 25 beans—not two and not a hundred. Or they might be asked, "About how long would it take to walk all the way around the softball field?" They will then take the walk, counting as they go to get a sense of how many minutes such a walk really takes. This will help them estimate in their heads, learning, for instance, that they need a certain amount of time to complete a particular task.

**Geometry.** Studying shapes provides children with a way of describing the world. ("The house has eight square windows and a roof that looks like a triangle.") Geometry also helps children see the relationship between shapes, such as when playing with blocks a child discovers that two right triangles make a square.

**Measurement.** In kindergarten and first grade particularly, kids become increasingly aware of size. They know who's tallest and who's shortest. They are learning that days are measured in seconds, minutes, and hours and that distances are measured in feet and miles.

**Statistics and probability.** Children learn to record facts, such as how many classmates have siblings or what each child's favorite snack is. Through such activities as taking classroom polls, children's understanding of similarities and differences and their grasp of what is real and what is not are enhanced.

**Helping your child understand numerical concepts**

You can help your child gain an understanding of mathematical concepts by:

*Using the language of math.* As you plan a day with your child, ask for suggestions about what to do first, next, and last. Note that dinner will be ready in "ten minutes." As you fold the wash, help your child match "pairs" of socks. In play, challenge your child to take a "double" or a "triple" jump.

*Play games that involve counting and number recognition.* Board games, especially ones that require a child to read dice and to count out moves, are a fun way to practice number skills. Card games, such as war, help hone your child's skill at knowing "less than" and "more than."

*Involve your child in shopping, saving, and spending.* Compare prices and sizes of items aloud as you shop with your child. Give your child some money to count and let her pay for small items herself. Encourage her to count out her change. Give her an allowance, letting her spend some and save some for larger purchases.

*Measure with your child regularly and record the results.* Measure toys, measure her room, measure her fingers and toes.

*Become a weather reporter.* With your child, make note of the day's temperature, the amount of rain or snowfall, even the speed of the wind.

*Make up number-guessing games.* Say, "I'm thinking of a number that's the same as the number of toes you have." Or, "I'm thinking of a number that's less than nine but more than seven." Let your child have a turn at leading the game, too.

## Is there a problem?

Many kindergartners and first-graders are perplexed when faced with written problems such as 2 + 2 = ——. If your child can understand the concept when working with real objects, such as taking two apples and placing them in a bowl with two other apples and concluding that there are now four apples, she's grasping the things she needs to know. Simply make sure that you provide her with plenty of practice in using real objects to understand math concepts. If she's doing things such as reversing numbers, don't worry; many children write backward 4's until the age of seven or so.

If, however, by the age of six, your child has difficulty recognizing the relationship between the numeral 4 and four objects or cannot see how triangles and rectangles relate, talk to her teacher. Learning disabilities that involve spatial skills or other math-based skills are generally more subtle than those involving language. If problems with math skills persist, be sure to have your child tested professionally so that she can receive the appropriate intervention.

### Your child's understanding of time

Your child is vaguely aware that you were once a child. As a new five-year-old, she may innocently ask if you had any dinosaurs as pets or why Grandma never had any children. The possibility that time (and dinosaurs) existed long before you did or that Grandma was once a young woman with a young child (you) are ideas that are simply too confusing to understand at this point.

As your child nears six, however, her understanding of time grows much deeper. She knows that the year goes through predictable seasons and that holidays and birthdays are repeated at set intervals. Her days are timed by activities—breakfast time, time for recess, time to go home, bedtime. Her memory is stronger and she can recall her last birthday party as she begins to prepare for her next one. She's coming to understand that "15 minutes" means about the same as "soon," though "tomorrow night" and "next year" may both seem like ages and ages from now. Though not ready yet to "tell time" from a clock (a skill that usually comes at about age seven or eight), your kindergartner or first-grader now has the language of time (seconds, days, years) and a growing awareness of the relationships between time concepts. To help your child gain a better understanding of time:

*Use time words and concepts as you go about activities.* Mention that you'll pick her up from a playdate "at 3:30. That's 30 minutes after three." Add that this is "one hour from now."

*Compare units of time to common activities.* If you tell your child that you'll be ready to go out to the park in "30 minutes," note that "That's the same amount of time as it takes to watch *Rugrats* on TV. Or when you say, "in three minutes," add, "about the time it takes you to brush your teeth."

*Have at least one analog clock in the house.* In addition to any digital clocks, make sure your child has access to a clock with a face and hour, minute, and second hands to help your child visualize the relationship between different times. A second hand helps her count out a whole minute—a big accomplishment.

*Play time games.* Close your eyes and try to guess when a minute is up. Then compare your guesses to the hands on the clock.

*Display a calendar.* Help your child count out how many days until or since an event. Cross off the days every night and see how many days have passed this month and how many are still to go. Point out the names of the days of the week and the months of the year, but don't insist that your child memorize them at the age of five. Most will learn them by six or seven.

*Don't insist on learning to tell time.* If your child is interested in learning to decipher a clock, buy a toy one to play with. But don't insist that your child actually try to learn to tell time just yet.

# Adapting to classroom experiences that may not suit her learning style

Often, when a child decides that school is "too hard" or "too easy," the real problem lies in a mismatch between the child's learning style and the learning environment.

Good teachers work hard to adapt the learning plan to each learner in the class, including a variety of lessons that tap into their charges' varied styles. There are times, however, when your child, who maybe works best in quiet surroundings, may be part of a boisterous and active lesson. Or your child who learns best by handling objects, may be asked to sit still during reading time. Having to sublimate their own natures to accommodate the needs of the classroom community is especially difficult for some children.

If your child is having serious problems keeping up or understanding the material, your first step should be to talk with the teacher. The teacher will be able to help work out a plan that will address your child's needs. You can also work to augment classroom activities at home. If your child seems stressed by sitting still a bit too much, make sure that her after-school hours include opportunities for her to run and play outdoors, leaving homework until after she's had a chance to cut loose.

## Learning disabilities and differences

If you suspect that your child is not developing at the same rate as her peers or seems to have particular difficulty with an aspect of her life at school, you may be concerned that she has a learning disability (LD). Your first reaction should not be one of alarm. Nearly 20 percent of American school-age children have some form of learning difficulty that prevents them from "getting" the material at an average or above-average rate. That doesn't in any way mean that a child with an LD can't learn or won't be able to excel. What an LD usually means is that the classroom situation and learning mode need to be adapted to suit the learner.

An LD can interfere with how your child approaches learning, retains what she learns, or expresses what she learns. Some LDs involve a problem with processing language. Others interfere with a child's ability to grasp mathematical concepts. Some LDs concern a child's emotional equilibrium. Early detection and intervention can keep an LD from affecting your child's self-esteem and attitude toward school and learning. Warning signs of learning disabilities include:

*A family history of LD.* If you or your spouse had particular difficulty learning to read and your child, too, seems confused by written language, she may have inherited the condition.

*Poor coordination and inefficient use of space.* Children with learning disabilities often are clumsy, regularly walking into furniture or knocking glasses of milk to the floor with their elbows. They also find it hard to button and zip clothing and to tie shoes. The difficulty negotiating space relates to their difficulty reading. They may not, in fact, be able to judge the spaces between words so that a task such as reading "See the brown bear" appears as "Seethebrownbear." Children with spatial difficulties also tend to avoid puzzles and blocks and to have trouble distinguishing between shapes, which, of course, also inhibits their ability to recognize letters.

*Extreme emotionalism.* Children who cry one minute and laugh the next, who feel picked on by their playmates, or who have wild mood swings may have neurological problems that prohibit them from processing information in a logical way.

*Oversensitivity to sensory cues.* Children who can't stand "itchy" clothes, bright lights, loud or high-pitched noises or who dislike being touched are less able to filter out distractions and have a much tougher time learning in a regular classroom setting.

If your child appears to be having a difficult time learning or concentrating, be sure that she is tested for lead poisoning. Early exposure to lead paint particles and dust has been proven to be a leading cause of learning and behavioral problems.

---

*A poor vocabulary.* Children who don't exhibit the same range of vocabulary as other kids their age may have deficits in hearing and speech development that tend to include difficulties with working well with other children.

If you suspect that your child has an LD, talk to her teacher or pediatrician. Your child's school district is required to offer free evaluations if a disability is suspected. If a disability is diagnosed, the school district must, according to the federal Individuals with Disabilities Education Act, provide appropriate intervention. Help may include any appropriate measure, from providing a once-a-week session with a speech pathologist to placing your child in a special learning environment for part or all of the school day.

Realize, too, that many, many children exhibit some of the signs of a learning disability at some point and that any one lag does not, in itself, signal a problem. Also remember that while a disability may mean that your child may need special help, it does not in any way reflect upon her intelligence or on her potential for future success in school. And getting her the help she needs early will decrease the chance of lasting ramifications.

### What to know about attention-deficit disorder (ADD) and attention-deficit hyperactivity disorder (ADHD)

There are three distinct stages in the development of an attention span. The first is called "exclusive," which describes how a typical infant rivets her attention on something she finds interesting. Most children move out of this phase as they enter toddlerhood. The second stage of attention-span development is called "inclusive." During this stage, a child flits from one focus point to another, easily distracted by any new stimuli. This stage is typified by a toddler's unbounded enthusiasm for anything new. Being stuck in this stage might lead to a diagnosis of ADD or ADHD. The third stage, which begins at around age five, marks a child's ability to shift her focus between different points of interest, to concentrate, and to block out extraneous stimuli.

Typically, a five-year-old can remain focused on things that interest her and quickly turn away from things that don't. Not every child who squirms in her seat at school, of course, has ADD or ADHD. For many kids, the inability to sit still is simply a result of a lack of maturity and lack of experience with a classroom setting. Not wanting to sit still through storytime may simply mean that a child doesn't like the story being told, not that she's hyperactive. When a child's ability to stay focused is *severely* hampered, however, she may be found to have ADD. When a lack of focus is combined with an inability to control her impulses, the diagnosis of ADHD might be made.

### Getting a diagnosis of ADD or ADHD

ADD or ADHD is diagnosed (and some say overdiagnosed) in nearly 10 percent of the population of school-age children. More boys than girls are considered to have one of these conditions. It is usually first suspected at three distinct periods of growth: among five- and six-year-olds who are just starting school, among fourth graders who had the condition earlier but who were able to compensate until the schoolwork became too complex, and among teens, again, who compensated well until schoolwork proved overwhelming.

If your child is suspected of having either ADD or ADHD, her physician will conduct a physical, including certain lab tests. The doctor will also have parents or teachers complete a questionnaire that explores the child's behavior over a period of time. If the diagnosis is leaning toward ADD or ADHD, additional physical or psychological tests may be recommended. The final diagnosis is made largely by ruling out other conditions, such as lack of sleep, poor nutrition, low thyroid, and emotional problems such as depression.

Treatment for ADD and ADHD usually, but not always, involves administering the prescription stimulant Ritalin, shown to be very effective for most kids, especially when combined with behavioral psychotherapy. Concerns over the use of this drug, however, have led researchers and parents themselves to search for other means—including a change in diet or behavior training alone—to help kids cope with this condition.

## YOU AND YOUR CHILD
## Understanding the connection between your and your child's learning styles

You might remember needing peace and quiet to do your own homework when you were a child. Even today, you may find it difficult to concentrate while the radio is playing softly in an adjoining room. It's only natural, you decide, that your child, too, needs quiet in order to learn. However, you may find that she sings to herself as she works on a word problem for math homework. Should you keep on insisting that your child do her homework quietly at her desk? Probably not.

Or perhaps you found schoolwork frustrating. You slogged through and expect that your child will, too. While there may be some wisdom in that approach, it, too, might be doing your child a disservice. Maybe, with help that might not have been available to you, your child can find school much more exciting and less frustrating than you did.

Even though your child may have inherited some physical and emotional traits from you, she's not your clone. Her learning style, like the color of her eyes, may be different from yours. What's important is to give your child a chance to find her most efficient means of accomplishing what she must. Let her experiment with ways of working—and tell her what you're up to: "Let's try different ways of doing homework—in the kitchen where the action is or in your room where it's quiet. Before dinner or in the evening, after we've eaten. With lots of breaks or straight through. With music on or not. Then we'll see what works best for you."

By giving your child the freedom to find what works best for her, she's learning another important lesson, too: that there are various ways to approach a problem and that by trying out different methods, she can discover the solution for herself. In addition, she learns that she's a vital partner in the learning process, not simply one who must learn what she is told to do and how she is told to do it.

## HELPING YOUR CHILD GROW
## Providing learning opportunities tailored to your child's style

Throughout your child's schooling, you are her number-one advocate, the person who knows her likes and dislikes, her strengths and her weaknesses best. Your role as your child's advocate is to help the teacher help your child, and to help your child help herself. You do that by sharing information with the teacher that supports your child's learning and by helping your child explore the many different ways in which she can learn. For instance, if your child is having difficulty understanding math concepts, and is therefore, clearly not a "mathematical/logical learner," you could try an approach that's suited to her style:

*If she loves to read, listen to stories, and talk about stories she has read.* Ask at your child's school or local children's library or bookstore for recommendations of books that use number concepts in the storyline, such as *6 Sticks* by Molly Coxe (Random House) and *The Berenstain Bears Catch the Bus* by Stan and Jan Berenstain (Random House).

**If she loves to draw and build with blocks.** Draw and build together, talking and demonstrating as you go about the various shapes involved, about how your drawn house has "four windows and two chimneys" and hers has "six windows and one door." Build a tower, each using a set number of blocks, saying something like "Let's see what we each can do with 12 blocks." Count them as you use them. Put them into different groups. "I used four for walls, three for a roof, and six for a fence." Encourage your child to describe her architecture, too.

**If your child is musically inclined.** Sing songs and recite poems that include numbers, such as "One, two, buckle my shoe . . ." Tap out beats as you say each number, counting from one to ten. Make up rhymes that help her remember.

**If your child likes a lot of activity.** Count while doing jumping jacks. Give her magnetic number forms to handle. Draw the numerals in the dirt with a stick. Count how long it takes for her to run from the bus stop to the corner.

**If your child has good people skills.** Invite friends over to play some board or card games that involve counting and recognizing numbers.

**If your child is introspective.** Help her think about numbers in terms of herself. How many fingers does she have? How many cousins? What shapes can she find in her bedroom? If she had two cookies and made three more, how many would she have in total?

## Helping your young student get organized

Certain children are more naturally inclined to order. Most five- and six-year-olds, however, need some help in getting organized. To help your child (and yourself, since it will fall to you to track down any misplaced homework) put some order into her life:

*Assign a place in your child's backpack for important papers.*
A special folder or see-through envelope can help you and your child
see immediately if there are any homework papers to be handed in
or school notices to be read at home.

*Keep a school calendar.* Mark dates immediately as you become
aware of them. Review the calendar nightly to see if any special
events are coming up, such as your turn to bring in school snacks,
a classmate's birthday party, or a school picnic.

*Teach the "toss out" habit.* Have your child regularly review her
backpack for excess paper, broken pencils, leftover lunch—things
that clutter her bag and are no longer useful.

*Teach the "double check" habit.* Each evening, have your child
review her schoolbag to make sure she has the requisite papers,
pencils, and other tools she'll need the next day. Are her pencils
sharpened? Are papers signed if need be?

*Have duplicate school supplies at home.* Have a designated
space at home for the supplies your child is likely to need for home
projects, such as scissors, paste, pencils, and a sharpener.

# Let me tell you a story

## Your child's reading and writing skills

**B**etween the ages of five and six, your child is moving from an understanding of language as a spoken means of communication to the knowledge that language can be extracted from written symbols. Whereas you once held the key to unlocking those symbols as you read to him, your child is now aware that the power to make a story leap from a page is about to be his, too.

Perched on the edge of the world of written language, your child has a huge speaking and an even larger listening vocabulary. More than likely, he is a chatterbox. With a speaking vocabulary of about 3,000 words (and 5,000 or more by the end of age six), he'll tell stories with gusto, though at this stage, he's still leaping from detail to detail, forgetting some essential parts along the way. He understands far many more words than he can use on his own and is drawn to the sounds of big words. As a listener, he's a bit uneven. He'll be alert to your whispers not intended for his ears, but he'll seem not to hear you when you ask him directly to pick up his toys.

By the age of five, your child is probably reading and writing, too. He can probably recognize his own printed name and familiar logos, such as McDonald's golden arches or Kmart's big red signs. He may create page after page of squiggles with a few odd letters thrown in to tell a story. Expressing himself by drawing is probably a favorite activity now. All of these activities are, in fact, aspects of literacy.

## DEVELOPMENTAL MILESTONE
## Readiness to read

Being "ready to read" is not a very complicated process. A child who loves books, loves being read to, enjoys new experiences, and has a thirst for learning is ready to read. Readiness is nothing more than a desire to unlock the treasure trove of information and entertainment that awaits once one is able to translate the symbols and understand the story.

There are, of course, emotional, physical, and intellectual skills that a child needs to go from readiness to reading. Emotionally, your child has to be enthusiastic about learning, be mature enough to understand that reading on his own involves practice and perseverance, and believe that he is capable of learning. Physically, he needs to have the eye coordination to track written symbols across and down a page and the auditory skills to distinguish between letter and word sounds so that he connects what he sees on a written page with what he hears. Intellectually, he needs to master decoding and comprehension skills.

Decoding is the ability to know, for instance, that the symbol *b* stands for the sound "buh" and is the first sound in words such as *ball* and *birthday*. Comprehension is the ability to make sense of words in sentences, paragraphs, and whole stories. It includes the ability to understand a passage that is heard or read; the ability to concentrate in order to follow a story's plot from beginning to end; and an understanding that different characters in a story may have different reasons for acting as they do. A reader also needs to be able to think logically about causes, effects, and implied meanings. For comprehension to occur, children need to make a connection between the words they hear and see and their own lives.

## The debate about reading instruction

Two different methods of teaching reading are called *phonics* and *whole language*. There has been strong debate among educators and parents over which type of instruction should be utilized to teach reading. Phonics, the ability to decode, is a skill, much like learning to balance is a skill that can support a child's ability to learn to ride a bike. Whole language, on the other hand, is a philosophy that proposes that children learn to listen, speak, read, and write in a natural way, by trial and error, and that immersion in reading builds a child's interest to allow fluency to take place. To use the bike-riding metaphor, whole language is akin to learning to ride by having lots of opportunities and experiences with bike riding.

Proponents of teaching reading primarily through phonics adhere to the idea that reading is based on sounding out words and that new readers learn to read by becoming adept at making the connection between letter symbols and letter sounds. They note that many children fail to learn merely by being exposed to literature and that children who cannot decode phonetically lack the key to unlocking written symbols.

Those less inclined toward a phonics-centric approach argue that a child who can sound out words does not necessarily comprehend them. Children who are taught primarily through phonics can also feel betrayed and unsure of what to do when they encounter phonetically irregular words such as *enough* or when they try to differentiate between words that have a similar appearance but very different sounds such as *low* and *cow* or similar sounds with different meanings, such as *end* and *and*. Furthermore, an overemphasis on phonics, they say, robs a new reader of the experience of enjoying literature, as it takes classroom time from the pleasure of reading and spends it instead on drill and practice with letter sounds. These arguments, however, do not diminish your child's need to learn phonics skills as *one* of a number of useful strategies he will use to read. Proponents of the whole-language approach to teaching reading also say that learning to read is a natural process, much like learning spoken language.

While phonics and whole language are often presented as opposing means of instruction, there is, in fact, no dichotomy between the two in the best classrooms. Early-education teachers understand that instruction in phonics skills as well as other reading strategies and an environment that is rich in literature underlie good reading instruction. The goal, after all, is for children to read with comprehension and to approach reading with a sense of enthusiasm.

**The strategies new readers use**
No one strategy works for all kids. To grasp the broad outline of a story as well as to uncover the meaning of individual words, most new readers use a combination of the following strategies and a range of underlying skills:

*Reading pictures.* Picture books provide new readers with very helpful cues about the story. You'll remember from when your child first began to choose his own books at the library or bookstore that he probably was drawn to books whose covers showed pictures that interested him: a dump truck, a baby animal, a picture of another child. When your child peruses the pictures in a story he's about to read or one that you're reading to him, he's giving himself an edge in predicting what the story will be about and is delighted when your words confirm that the story tells more about the picture.

**Being curious.** A book that inspires a new reader to wonder "What will happen next?" encourages a child. Your new reader may attempt to answer the question by listening intently as you or his teacher reads. He may scan the pictures for more clues. Or he may read any familiar words in the text and use his knowledge of the characters or the plot thus far to figure out the meaning of the words he cannot recognize.

**Guessing.** A new reader uses picture, story, and initial-letter clues to guess the meaning of unfamiliar words. If, for instance, your child can recognize the words *the, dog, is, a,* and *hat,* and sees a picture of a dog wearing a hat, he can guess the meaning of the word *wearing* in the sentence "The dog is wearing a hat." He may use his knowledge of letter sounds to know that the word he needs to guess begins with the "wa" sound, so he doesn't guess "The dog is *buying* a hat" or "The dog is *trying on* a hat."

**Using sound and context clues.** Rhyming and repetition also help a child guess the meaning of an unfamiliar word. For instance, if you read "Ants *go* down be*low* and bees *fly* way up ———." Your child will guess that the unknown word is *high* because he's anticipating a rhyme as well as expecting the unknown word to make sense in context. Or if he's reading or listening to a story with a refrain, such as "He huffed and he puffed and he blew the house down," your new reader will recognize where in the story to repeat these words himself.

**Memorizing.** A new reader often returns repeatedly to a favorite book, learning each time he encounters the book that the same symbols bear the same meaning. Though he may recognize the words *The Cat in the Hat,* each time in that familiar book, he may not recognize the word *cat* in another context at first. Eventually, however, he makes the connection that the letters *c-a-t* stand for the word *cat* wherever he sees them.

***Using phonics.*** Connecting letter symbols to sounds is a very useful approach, especially when decoding a phonetically regular but unfamiliar word that is not clear from the picture clues or from other story content. Most new readers gain immeasurably by learning phonics skills. A child who knows the correlation between the letters *n-a-m-e* and the sounds that each letter represents can figure out the word *name* in a sentence such as "I know my name."

***Recalling experiences.*** Your child's everyday experiences lay much of the groundwork for his ability to read. If, for instance, he encounters the words *elephant* and *tusks* in a sentence, any real-life experiences he has had with elephants, such as visits to the zoo, will help engage him in the story and help him connect any picture or letter clues to the meanings of these words.

## Reading in the classroom

Children arrive in the classroom, whether it's a kindergarten or first-grade class, with varying levels of reading ability. To engage children of differing skills, good teachers use a variety of teaching methods and types of activities, including:

***Listening.*** Daily whole-class and small-group experiences give children a chance to listen to good literature and to respond to its meaning. A teacher might read a book aloud and then ask the class to talk about it, answering such questions as "Why did a character do what he did?" or "What do you think will happen next?"

***Reading together.*** Using "big books," books designed for new readers that have easy-to-read words set in large type for the whole class or reading group to see, teachers encourage children to read along together as the teacher points to the words.

***Small-group reading.*** A few times each week, the teacher groups children into small reading groups based on the children's needs.

One group might be encouraged to read independently, while another works with the teacher on letter sounds, and a third works with an aide on one-on-one read-aloud sessions.

*Independent reading.* Children are encouraged to choose books themselves from the classroom library to read on their own.

*Skill-building exercises.* These might be done as whole-class or small-group activities, in which the teacher reviews reading strategies.

## CONFLICT
# The cost of learning to read

There are two, often subconscious, roadblocks to becoming a fluent reader that have nothing to do with your child's abilities. Even if he's thriving on the challenge of reading to himself, he knows that there's a price to pay for his growing competence. The books he's able to handle alone aren't nearly as interesting as those designed to be read to him. The plots and vocabulary are less complex, the stories are necessarily less involved, and the sentences are shorter. To some kids, reading such beginner books is simply boring and they'd rather not read at all if these simple books are all they can handle. Further, his own voice, if he stumbles on the words when reading aloud, doesn't sound nearly as delightful as yours. After years of enjoying listening to you read him stories, he may sense that

**Did you know?**
• On average, bilingual children learn to read slightly ahead of their monolingual peers. Researchers surmise that children in bilingual households are more comfortable with the knowledge that language can take on many forms, so that when faced with written words, they see them as just another means of communicating.
• Children of working single parents have a much larger vocabulary on average than their peers. Researchers believe that this is because the parent spends more time in one-to-one communication with the child rather than in conversations with another adult.

once he's able to read himself, the lovely ritual of your reading to him will come to an end.

By continuing to read to him, you will greatly allay his fears as well as continue to improve his reading and listening skills. And when you're reading those books that are beyond his independent reading level, encourage him now and then to read a sentence that you know he can handle. He'll be surprised and happy to find that although he may not be ready to read all of *Treasure Island* on his own, he is capable of reading some of it.

## Is there a problem?

Children who are learning to read often stumble over words, just as a new walker stumbles as he makes his way across a room. The territory is unfamiliar, and it can be difficult to keep track of all the rules of reading, such as stopping at periods and remembering that the letter c can make both the sound heard in *cup* and that in *cereal*. Continue to offer encouragement and lots of exposure to writing. Talk to your child about what you're reading to him to ascertain whether he's having difficulty understanding the ideas in the story or if the problem is more of a decoding one. If, despite your continued patient guidance and reading experiences, your child doesn't seem to be catching on, there are some steps you can take to provide him with more practice. If decoding is the problem, play word and sound games that give him more exposure to letter sounds and shapes. If comprehension is causing problems, help your child listen closely for clues in the story to help him understand what the story is about. Discuss how the title of the story helps him make good guesses about it. Talk about the pictures. What parts of the story do they illustrate? Ask questions about what happens first, next, and last. It's essential that you also address the problem with his teacher or pediatrician. You may want to have his hearing and eyesight checked as well, since the roots of undiagnosed language difficulties often lie in physical problems. Testing to see if he has a language-based learning disability is also appropriate. Getting the right help as early as possible can make the difference between a short-term problem and one that affects him for years.

## Learning to write

Because writing and reading go hand in hand, children should be encouraged to write right from the start. Since children's drawings are their first attempt at written communication, most children are already proficient "writers" when they enter the classroom. So writing instruction often is integrated with art and builds on what children already know about telling a story rather than assuming that writing must include words alone.

Now, at age five or six, your child is well aware that the squiggles and dots need to take a certain form to be understood by you or any other readers. He may have begun to make the transition from scrawling to writing by adding a drawn *C* to his picture of a cat. From there, he may write *C——T* or even *CAT* to label his picture. When encouraged to "tell a story" about his picture, your child goes on to use what he knows about letter sounds and the conventions of writing that he has observed in his reading to write, "Mi dg is blk. His nm is Jm. Hs a gd dg. i love hm." (My dog is black. His name is Jim. He's a good dog. I love him.) Because the consonant sounds are more pronounced, he'll rely more heavily on them than on vowel sounds to get his message across. Unrestrained by the need for correct spelling or punctuation, he feels free to continue his story-telling in writing.

## Writing in the classroom

When children are just learning to write, the emphasis is on formulating their ideas and transferring those ideas to paper. Teachers don't insist on standardized spelling and punctuation at this early stage any more than you would have insisted on correct pronunciation when your child was a toddler just learning to speak. This emphasis on the story allows your child to build confidence in his ability to communicate using written language. The mechanics are learned as a means of strengthening their stories, so children are eventually motivated to learn the conventions of spelling and mechanics in a context that makes sense.

In first-grade classrooms there will be more emphasis on spelling and punctuation. Children might be given lists of words to spell or may be encouraged to create their own spelling dictionaries using words that are personally meaningful to them.

While some parents are concerned that traditional spelling does not get enough attention, researchers have found that most children who write confidently and often in kindergarten through second grade do indeed become, by third or fourth grade, fluent spellers. By the age of eight or so, they are better equipped to understand the rules and have had more experience with seeing standard spelling in their reading.

## The drawing-writing connection

Ironically, the need to master reading and writing makes your child particularly passionate about artwork now. More than ever, your kindergartner or first-grader wants to spend hours drawing and coloring, cutting and pasting. These familiar forms of expression remind him that he is able to communicate what's on his mind without having to struggle to follow any confusing rules.

Just months ago, your five-year-old could ad-lib and recreate the meaning of his drawing until he was satisfied. For instance, he might draw a bluebird and tell you a long, involved story about it, using a rich vocabulary and an uncompromised imagination. If you pointed to a tree in his drawing and asked, "Does the bird live in the tree?" he would add a new story element, detailing how the bird hides her nest in the tallest branches. Now, writing means that he has fewer options about what to say about his picture. The story becomes fixed, unchangeable, once he is working with the constraints of words he can write. He may become frustrated by the way written words limit his story.

It's important at this time not to focus all of your child's attention on his need to learn to read and write. Even if he's proud of the writing he's doing in the classroom, there's no need to suggest that each drawing he creates at home include a written component. Continue to encourage his artistic expression for its own sake, giving him the continued joy of visibly and verbally sharing his stories with you.

## Supporting your child's comfort with writing

While reading begins with your child responding to words and ideas written by others, writing begins with ideas that your child brings to the table. Therefore, a good place to help your child become increasingly comfortable with written language is by encouraging writing. You can help your child boost his writing skills in a number of ways:

*Transcribe his stories.* Let him dictate his stories for you to write to accompany his pictures.

*Encourage a large written vocabulary.* Urge your child to use words from his speaking vocabulary as he writes, rather than limit himself to words he's learned to spell. Let him know that you're available to help him spell any word he wants to use, but don't discourage him from using invented spelling if that helps him proceed with his storytelling.

*Use technology.* Invest in a child-appropriate word-processing program so that your child doesn't have to concern himself with his handwriting when he wants to write. Consider getting a voice-activated word processor that allows your child to dictate his story to the computer. Let your child dictate stories into a tape recorder for playing back later.

*Encourage letter writing.* Have him send his drawings and accompanying words to his grandparents and friends. Let him make birthday cards rather than using store-bought ones. Write letters to one another at home. Pack a note such as "I hope you like this cookie" with your child's lunch and have a space on the note for your child to check "yes" or "no" to give to you as a written reply. Buy picture postcards for your child to send to his friends.

**Have fun with handwriting.** Some kids struggle mightily to draw their letters neatly. Help take some of the pressure off by having fun with drawing letters. For instance, your child could draw an *A* with wings to symbolize the word *angel*. Or he can make a butterfly wing with a *B* and a cat's tail with a curled *C*.

**Create a personal book.** Using old photos, drawings, or other art supplies, help your child create a personalized book. He could illustrate and write a book about a favorite subject, such as monsters. Or he could create a memory book about a recent vacation or about his pet cat.

## HELPING YOUR CHILD GROW
## Raising a reader

It's vital to remember that reading is a developmental issue, just like walking. The child who learned to walk at 8 months is not now a better walker than the child who didn't take his first steps until 14 months. Likewise, the child who reads at age five will not necessarily be a better reader than one who doesn't begin to read until age seven. No matter when a child is ready to read, however, he needs your support. To raise an enthusiastic reader:

**Read aloud every day.** Even 15 minutes of enjoying books together each day can lay the groundwork. More is even better. Read while you're waiting in line at the grocery. Read on the bus. Have at least one daily ritual of reading, such as a bedtime story.

**Get cozy with reading.** Have a special comfortable reading chair in which you and your child can cuddle up while you read to him or while he reads to you. Make a "reading tent" by draping a sheet over some chairs to read a high-adventure story. Read by flashlight in a darkened room. Read a story about olden times by candlelight.

***Ensure that basic letter skills are falling into place.*** Help your child learn to recognize uppercase and lowercase letters. Play games to help him learn the sounds of each letter. To help the lessons about letter sounds click, try to find words that are personally meaningful to your child with which to connect letter sounds and symbols. For example, if he loves helping you cook, teach that *a* is for *applesauce, b* is for *bake.* As you read together, help him see that sometimes letters go together to make new sounds, such as *ch* in *cherry;* that the same letter can make different sounds, such as *c* in *car* and *circle;* and that two letters can make the same sound, such as *c* sounding like *k* in *castle* or like *s* in *cereal.*

***Build a home library.*** Your child should have his own books in a readily accessible place. He also needs to have favorite stories available to him to read again and again.

***Visit the public library.*** Make a habit of visiting the library for your child to pick out new books weekly. Once your child can write his own name, he can get his own library card, a passport to reading that he'll feel proud to own.

***Talk about books.*** Compare characters and plots. Ask what he likes and doesn't like about different stories. See if you both can come up with different possible endings for a story or different names for the characters.

***Take "word walks."*** As you and your child are going about your day, play games such as finding in a store all the words that begin with the letter *s.* Or see how many words you can find that have three letters. Think about rhyming words. If you see a stop sign, see how many words you and your child can name that rhyme with *stop.*

***Tape stories.*** Tape yourself or an older sibling reading a favorite book to your prereader. Ask grandparents to record themselves reading a book and to send along the tape and the book for your child to read along. Let your child tape himself reading a favorite story.

***Be a reading model.*** Let your child see you enjoying books. Discuss what you're reading for your own pleasure with him.

***Point out the usefulness of reading.*** New readers are sometimes unaware that reading is not just for enjoyment or for storytelling. Let your child know that you read instructions describing how to put together his bicycle, that recipes help you know how to bake a cake, or that a written schedule lets you know when your plane will take off. Let your child peruse the menu at a restaurant or the list of coming attractions at the local theater.

***Make connections between reading and other entertainment.*** If a favorite TV show or character is based on a book, read the book and see how alike or different they are. Rent video versions of storybooks and both read the book and view the video. If there's a stage production of a children's book at a local school or library, take your child to the performance.

### Making the most of reading time
When you sit down to read to your child, the focus, of course, needs to be on the pleasure of you, your child, and the book at hand. But now that your child is ready to become a reader, there are things you can do as you read to him to further his understanding of decoding and to aid in his comprehension.

***Let your child review a new book, cover to cover.*** Encourage him to look over the pictures. Ask him to predict what the book will be about.

**Point out the author's name and the title of the book.** Show your child where they appear on the cover and help him find the author's name and title of the book repeated on the inside. Review any other nonstory parts of the book, such as a table of contents or an index. Let your child know the purpose of each.

**Go on a punctuation hunt.** Offer a brief lesson in how a story is formatted. Point out that all the sentences begin with a capital letter and end with a period, exclamation point, or question mark. After identifying a question mark, ask your child to find another in the book. Show your child how you stop at a period and pause at a comma. When you see a passage of dialogue, point out that the quotation marks around the words help readers know that a character is speaking.

**Stop occasionally to ask questions.** As you read, ask questions like "What do you think will happen next?" or "Why do you think the character did that?" If your child prefers not to have the storytelling interrupted, save the questions until after you've finished reading.

**Point out words that begin with the same letter and sound.** When you come across the word *river,* for instance, ask your child to find other words, such as *red* or *robin,* that start with the same letter sound.

**After reading, compare the book you've just read to others.** Does your child know any other books by the same author? Any other books about the same character or type of character?

**Tips for helping your child read aloud confidently**
When your child is first beginning to read independently, he'll want to show off his skill to you by reading aloud. What do you do if your child hesitates over a word or says a word that's not correct?

When your child stumbles over a new word, you may simply want to provide the word and let him continue. At least some of the time, however, help him find a strategy for figuring it out: Ask him what word might make sense in the story. Have him look at the pictures if they provide appropriate clues. If the word is phonetically regular, see if he can use his knowledge of word sounds to sound it out. If he has read the word on another page but doesn't recognize it now, point out the previous use.

If, while reading a sentence such as "The bird built a house in the tree," your child misreads "a home" instead of "a house," just ignore it since the word makes sense in the sentence. If he misreads "horse" for "house," however, gently interrupt him and ask him if "horse" makes sense in the sentence "The bird built a horse in the tree."

Memorizing a book helps many children feel confident about reading aloud because they can perform not only the words but the intonations of the story. Don't be concerned that memorizing is not really reading. It is a useful way for many kids to connect to written language. To hone his reading skills, encourage your new reader to read to a younger child who will love the attention. Your child will benefit from seeing just how much more he can do with a storybook than a toddler or preschooler can, whether or not he's actually reading the story as written.

The important thing is to let your child feel the success of reading, not to get caught up in the frustration that can accompany learning to read.

**Recognizing reading difficulties**
While just about every child can and does learn to read by the age of eight, some children do experience some real difficulty. Sometimes reading hesitation is simply a matter of development. A child who's not ready to read independently at six may well be ready by seven. Continuing to read to your child and supporting his desire to read while he learns will help most later readers reach their stride. Sometimes, however, a child's difficulty with

learning to read is due to an underlying emotional or physical problem, including vision problems. If your child shows any of the following difficulties, talk to his teacher or pediatrician about having him evaluated so that he can receive early intervention:

♦ Squints or gets tired and teary-eyed when doing tasks that require close visual attention.

♦ Refuses to try to learn to read, either deciding that it's "too hard" or not important enough to attempt.

♦ Doesn't seem to make the connection between letters and sounds.

♦ Makes wild guesses about what a word might be in the context of a sentence.

♦ Cannot retell a story reasonably well, giving, for instance, the main plot lines and the names of the main characters.

♦ Cannot use spoken or written language to tell or retell a story.

♦ Often confuses letters and sounds and, beyond the age of seven, reverses letters and reverses the order of letters in words when attempting to spell. For instance, spelling *the* as *het* or *on* as *no*. Reversals in writing by young writers are not a cause for concern. Most five- and six-year-olds at least occasionally write a letter backwards. When this persists, however, it may be a symptom of a reading disorder known as dyslexia.

If your child has a learning disability that interferes with his ability to read, get help at the earliest opportunity. Your child is entitled to appropriate intervention provided by your local school district.

## Classic books for new readers

- *Best Friends for Frances* by Russell Hoban (HarperCollins)
- *Frog and Toad Are Friends* by Arnold Lobel (HarperCollins)
- *George and Martha* by James Marshall (Houghton Mifflin)
- *Little Bear* by Else Homelund (HarperCollins)
- *The Little Engine That Could* by Watty Piper (Grosset & Dunlap)
- *The Runaway Bunny* by Margaret Wise Brown (HarperCollins)
- *Where the Wild Things Are* and *In the Night Kitchen* by Maurice Sendak (HarperCollins)

Great anthologies to have on hand for reading to your five- or six-year-old include:
- *Ready ... Set ... Read! The Beginning Reader's Treasury* edited by Joanna Cole (Doubleday)
- *Ready ... Set ... Read—and Laugh! A Funny Treasury for Beginning Readers* edited by Joanna Cole (Doubleday)
- *The 20th Century Children's Book Treasury* edited by Janet Schulman (Knopf)

# I am what I am

## Your child's personality and gender identity

Stepping into a playground of five- and six-year-olds is like entering a kaleido-scope. The kids form a brilliant swirl of activity, but, upon closer inspection, you see that the scene is really made up of disparate parts. Some children are busily engaged in rough-and-tumble sports. Some stand off to the sidelines, enjoying the action going on around them, but content not to join in just yet. Others are gathered in groups of two or three, chatting away or simply playing quietly side by side. A few may seem melded to their parents or caregivers. And still others may be like jagged edges of glass, studiously avoided by all the other kids.

The differences among children reach much further than their obvious differences in appearance. The ways in which children approach their world is to a great degree forged by their environments and prior experiences. The child who is raised to be confident tends indeed to act with confidence. The child who has been given the opportunity to form strong friendships is far more likely to engage in social play. And the child who has been bullied tends to seek out others to bully. Yet you're also likely to see the child of a very social parent act in a reticent manner, shying away from the play around her. Or you may see the child of a quiet parent leading a group of her peers in a boisterous game. What you're seeing is the overriding inborn temperaments of the children shining through.

The interplay of environment, inborn personality, and gender create your child's unique personality. You have been providing the environment that has helped her blossom into the person she has become. And your responses to her continue to determine how her personality will keep developing. Understanding the components that affect who your child is will help you bring out the best in her as she faces new experiences and obstacles.

From the time your child first smiled at all who approached her—or belted out a wail to signal that she'd rather not be introduced to everyone who came her way—you had clues to your child's inborn temperament. While her experiences in the first five or six years of her life have clearly helped shape her behavior, her inborn personality is what will determine her initial reactions to new situations. For instance, aided by your nurturance, your shy toddler may have learned to be socially adept in her small nursery school and preschool classes, especially once she had a chance to become familiar with the environment and people around her. As a new kindergartner or first-grader, however, you may see a return to her shy ways, at least until she's had time to adjust to the new environment.

## DEVELOPMENTAL MILESTONE
# Strong identification with same-sex parent

During this period of your child's life, she is struggling mightily to forge her identity, to fit in while standing out. She adapts her behavior to the environment, learning step by step what it means, for instance, to be a schoolkid. She adjusts her expectations of herself based largely on what you, her teachers, and her peers think. She's aware that she's growing up, physically and emotionally. She has a level of introspection that allows her to judge her own reactions to the world around her. She's incredibly aware that she is changing. By the age of five, your child has figured out that one aspect of who she is *is* fixed—her gender. With the same gusto with which she approaches all of life's expectations now, your child embraces her sense of herself as a member of a certain sex.

Girls at ages five and six can become stereotypically "girly," wanting to wear dresses and frilly clothes, for instance, and behaving in ways they deem appropriately feminine. Tutus and tiaras are the fashions of the day. Boys want to be just like Dad, and to behave in ways they perceive to be masculine. They may, however, far exceed Dad when it comes to being macho.

To solidify their newfound identities as male or female, children this age go through a period of having an extremely strong attachment to their same-sex parent. Boys may become defiant of Mom's authority, saying, for instance, "I don't care what you say. I'm asking Dad." Girls may treat their dads as interesting, but not terribly important, people. Since this follows a period in which boys declare that they want to marry Mom and girls insist that they're going to marry Dad, the sudden turn toward the same-sex parent can leave the opposite-sex parent feeling a bit hurt and rejected.

It's extremely important that parents respond with a combination of grace and support for each other at this time. Dad needs to back up Mom rather than to encourage his son to try to exclude her, and Mom needs to back up Dad as well.

There's no need to try to force your child to concede that his or her gender is not the best one, though, or to try to prevent your child from occasionally engaging in stereotypical behavior. For instance, while you should continue to offer your daughter lots of opportunities for physical play and nonsexist toys such as building blocks, there's no need to ban the Barbies. Likewise, if your son is particularly drawn to superhero play and games that test his physical prowess, don't insist that he stage a tea party instead. At this age, as they are solidifying their sense of themselves as people of a certain gender, the stereotypical actions in which children are engaged act as a sort of proof to them that they are, immutably, who they are. In the midst of so many other changes that they are experiencing, their status as boys or girls is extremely comforting.

| If your child... | Do say | Don't say |
|---|---|---|
| says, "All boys are dumb" | "Dad's a boy, and he's not dumb." | "I know what you mean." |
| wants to play only stereotypical games | "Let's play a game of Chutes and Ladders together." | "No more playing princess. That's not realistic." |
| refuses to play with opposite-sex kids | "It's better to learn to get along with everyone even if you prefer girls right now." | "Girls should only play with other girls because boys are too rough." |

## CONFLICT
## Pride in and a sense of privacy about her body

It's a rare five-year-old who doesn't insist at least once in a while that you squeeze her upper arm to marvel at her muscles. Girls and boys alike are aware and proud of their developing strength. Sprouting taller each day, your child is thrilled that she has grown enough to reach the books on the high shelves and that her legs may stretch to reach the floor when she sits at the kitchen table.

By six, your child may show you the first glimmer of what her teenage years may be like as she spends a bit more time in front of the mirror, combing her hair "just so." She becomes aware of her walk, her stance, and may emulate the swagger of an admired classmate. Her whole being shouts out, "Look at me!" Her pride in her physical being is almost palpable.

So, you may be surprised to find that your five- or six-year-old, who so recently ran through the house naked without even a thread of embarrassment, may now primly hide behind a washcloth as you rinse her hair in the bath. Her newfound modesty, especially around opposite-sex parents and siblings, is a healthy sign that she understands that she's no longer a baby. Her recognition that her private parts are, well, private, extends to her feelings about your modesty, too. It's important from this age onward that you and other adults respect your child's need for privacy, including not appearing naked or even semidressed around her and not invading her space when she's not dressed. Eventually, boys will feel more comfortable in stages of undress around their fathers and other males, as will girls with their moms and other females.

If your child shows no signs of embarrassment at being naked at this age, it's now time to encourage her to cover up. Be sure not to shame her, but let her know that as a big kid, she's expected to be dressed in public.

### Talking to your child about sexuality

At five, your child more or less withdraws from the highly personal interest in things sexual that she probably had at age four. At four, she was remarkably curious about her body parts, especially those that specifically made her a girl. She was curious to compare her girl parts to any boy's parts, and her friends of both sexes were eager to comply. But at the age of five, even as issues concerning gender-related behavior move to the forefront, your child's interest in her own and her friends' sexuality wanes considerably. She has likely internalized the notion that her sexuality is private, and she will go to great lengths to conceal her private parts from public view. Keeping a distance from people of the opposite sex helps both boys and girls establish that they belong to a group of others just like them.

At six, however, your child's interest in her own and others' sexuality reemerges. She's incredibly curious about sexuality, not just gender differences. She may wonder where babies come from in a much more scientific and logical way than she wondered at the age of four or five.

Your child's acceptance of her sexuality and her future emotional health regarding her sexuality is quite dependent now on your reactions to her curiosity. By now, your child should know the proper names for her body parts. Her questions should be encouraged and need to be answered honestly. When, for instance, she asks you where babies come from, don't get flustered or in any way indicate that the question is embarrassing or inappropriate. Answer simply something like, "Babies grow inside a special place in mommies called a uterus or womb right below the stomach." Don't go overboard with long, involved explanations, however, which would only serve to confuse her. Always express to your child that you're glad she asked her question and follow up with, "Is there anything else you'd like to know?" to let her know that she's free to continue to bring her questions to you.

If you find your child involved in playing doctor or other games to satisfy her curiosity, don't overreact. Explain to the children involved that their curiosity is natural, but that viewing or touching each others' private parts is not allowed. Be sure to let your child know that she has a right to refuse to allow anyone (except the doctor during an exam) to make her feel uncomfortable by looking at or touching her private parts.

## YOU AND YOUR CHILD
# Dealing with your child's temperament

Your innate temperament is part of what makes you *you*. And how you react to your child's reflects an aspect of your natural temperament. If your personality is similar to your child's, you may be in a better position to understand her, but the similarities in your approach to life may keep you from exploring the options fully as you help your child navigate the world. For instance, if you're a slow-to-warm-up parent of a slow-to-warm-up child, you may be very sensitive to your child's shyness. While this will help you understand this trait, it might also prevent you from helping your child to counter her fears and to forge ahead in her social life. Likewise, an easygoing parent and an easygoing child might seem like a perfect fit. But if you're too easygoing, you might have difficulty teaching your child to be appropriately assertive.

Challenging personalities can create a volatile mix between parent and child. Unchecked, your own strong personality can combine with that of your child to create a nearly constant power struggle. With the benefit of maturity, however, you can greet your child's intense personality with a kind of acceptance that others may not be able to show her, a particularly needed response for a child whom others may find overwhelming. It's very important that you not set up your child for defiance, a situation that could happen if you don't take pains to work with and around your child's intense nature.

Having opposing temperaments creates other issues. For example, if you're easygoing and socially comfortable yourself, it might be hard to accept your slow-to-warm-up child's need to hold back. Your own easy nature could make you too safe a harbor, however, and prevent you from helping your child learn to mingle. Rather than growing impatient with your sensitive, slow-to-warm-up child, work with her to find strategies for taking steps toward sociability. If your temperament is more restrained than that of your challenging child, you might likely ask, "Where did this child come from?" Having a child who's so very different in temperament isn't easy. But a change in *your* perspective—learning to see your demanding child as a fun and worthwhile challenge—can do wonders for your relationship. One of your main objectives will be to maintain your authority with a child with such a strong will. It's important to be confident and consistent when disciplining your challenging child. Wavering or giving in just to keep the peace would result in more, not less, conflict. Your child will be happier and more cooperative when she knows that you're in charge.

If you're the one with the strong personality and your child is either easy or slow-to-warm-up, it wouldn't be hard for you to overwhelm your child emotionally. Be especially alert to your child's desire to please you and be sure that she learns to consider her own feelings, not just yours. When encouraging your easy or slow-to-warm-up child's independence, be aware of the need to nurture, allowing her to retreat to you for comfort. Realize that, unlike you, she doesn't need to be in charge when playing with her friends, so don't disparage her ability to compromise. Pushing your easygoing child too hard or being domineering with her will undermine her confidence and limit her ability to become a good decision maker.

## Dealing with a sensitive child

Some children are hypersensitive to criticism and to feelings of being left out. If your child bursts into tears too easily, you can help her gain the control she needs while building her confidence in handling situations that unravel her.

***Don't chastise her for her tears.*** The pain your child feels is real, even if you can't understand how a matter that seems trivial to you can be so important to her. Telling her to "toughen up" only makes her feel more alone and vulnerable. Instead, ask her to calm down and tell you what's troubling her.

***Don't offer rewards to stop crying.*** Offering bribes could create a cycle in which, unconsciously, your child finds benefits in her continued tearful responses to hurts and disappointments.

***Empathize, but offer other responses.*** Let her know that there are other ways to handle her feelings. Say something like, "I know you're upset. Let's think of ways to handle feeling this way that don't include tears." Suggest that your child address the issue directly, learning to say, for instance, "I don't like it when you take the crayon I was using," instead of crying or becoming hysterical about the situation. Teach her to resolve conflicts and to settle her feelings by counting to 5 or 10 before reacting emotionally, giving herself time to think about more mature responses before she acts.

***Observe tear triggers.*** Keep a mental record of the occasions that bring on the tears. Does she cry more readily when she's tired or hungry? If physical needs reduce her ability to handle frustration or hurts, take care of the underlying problem, making sure that she doesn't skip meals or get too little sleep. Do certain playmates bring on more tears? Consider cutting down on their get-togethers or providing more than the usual supervision to keep emotions from spinning out of control.

***Role-play.*** When your child is calm, practice scenarios that cause her to cry. For instance, if she cries when a playmate insists on using the best props for dress-up play, work with her to find possible solutions. Maybe she could divide the props fairly before playmates arrive. Maybe she could set a time limit on how long each child gets to use each item.

***Discipline gently.*** A sensitive child can be handled best with a firm "That's not acceptable." But a more resilient kid may need more discipline to get her attention. You may have to raise your voice or give her a time-out, for example.

## Avoiding gender stereotyping

Few parents set out to limit their children's potential, yet subtle forms of sexual stereotyping do just that. Parents of boys, for instance, may be less patient if their sons show fear when learning to swim. Parents of girls may be less encouraging of their physical prowess. The results are boys who don't get enough nurturance and girls who get too much. To give both boys and girls the best chance of developing fully:

*Watch what you say.* Statements like "Big boys don't cry" or "It's not ladylike to get dirty" limit a child's sense of who she is and what she can do.

*Watch how you play.* Are you more likely to offer to toss a ball to your son or play house with your daughter? While children do indeed often gravitate to gender-stereotypical activities, all kids need exposure to lots of types of play. Nonsexist toys such as art materials, blocks, and board games give all children opportunities to create and to work together. Offering opposite-gender toys, such as a tool set to a girl or a potholder-weaving kit to a boy, gives both the opportunity to develop new skills.

*Don't focus on girls' appearances.* All children love to hear that they look good. However, regularly praising girls for their pretty hair or nice outfits sends the message that they are valued more for their looks than for their actions.

*Don't assume.* When digging in the garden, for instance, don't assume that your daughter will run from a squirming worm while your son will be interested in getting a closer look. Don't assume that your daughter will help out in the kitchen while your son assists in washing the car. Offer all children a chance to approach what's before them without trepidation.

**Watch for stereotypes in the media.** Be savvy about what you let your child watch on TV and at the movies. Make sure both boys and girls are exposed to images of sensitive males and heroic females.

**Discuss feelings with boys and action with girls.** Boys are trained early on to pay attention to action while ignoring the emotional impact of the action, while the opposite is true for girls. When reading a story such as *The Three Little Pigs,* ask your son how the pigs must have felt when the wolf approached. Ask your daughter about the strategies the pigs used to protect themselves.

# Who's in charge here?

## Disciplining your child

At five, your child is so intent on showing you how good he can be, you'll usually be hard-pressed to find much about his behavior to complain about, especially if your expectations are realistic. No, you can't really expect him to sit still in a fancy restaurant for two hours without fidgeting or worse, but if you remember to compliment him on his good manners at the dinner table at home, he'll reward you with an evening of stellar behavior. In other words, within the confines of what he is *able* to do, he will do everything he can to please you or other important adults in his life.

But for the next year and a half or so after he reaches five-and-a-half, you'll need to develop some new strategies for encouraging positive behavior while limiting the negative. What worked when your child was two or four may not be appropriate or even possible now. You may not, for example, be able to lift your 40-pound five-and-a-half-year-old to remove him from the scene as you did when he was a 20-pound toddler. And if he's been given time-outs for misbehavior since he was three, this approach may have lost its meaning by now.

On the plus side, you've got more tools at your disposal now than you had when he was younger. Logic can work wonders, as your child is ready to learn the reasons behind your decisions. His more sophisticated sense of humor will allow you to diffuse situations more readily than you could in the past. He's developing a conscience that stands in for you as the arbiter of right and wrong. *(For more on moral development, see pages 130–41.)* He's increasingly capable of being patient and will, therefore, be responsive to deal making and trade-offs for cooperative behavior.

While disciplining a five- or six-year-old is, in many ways, far easier than disciplining a tantrum-throwing toddler or an impulsive preschooler, your child's opportunities for getting himself into trouble are expanding. At school, the demands on him are higher than they've ever been. Adjusting to the strictures that come with being part of a class can be difficult for some kids. New rules, after all, invite new misbehaviors. Moreover, he's far more exposed to children whose value systems may differ vastly from yours. Just as he enjoys trying on costumes and acting like a pirate or superhero, he's likely to experiment with behaviors he learns from other children. He may be startled to find out that what seems to be acceptable behavior for others is not so for him, or that what is acceptable in your home doesn't meet the expectations of a playmate's parent or a teacher.

## DEVELOPMENTAL MILESTONE
# Recognizing that families have different rules

Up to about age five-and-a-half, your child has been relatively unaware of differences between your family's way of doing things and other families' habits. Certainly, he saw that families looked different from one another and had varying numbers of members. But because he observed these differences while with familiar people or in familiar situations, he was not particularly struck by the differences.

Now, with his social network expanding, he's more likely to venture out on his own—to play for a few hours at a time with friends in their homes, for instance. Without you or his teacher setting the tone, he becomes acutely aware that a parent in another household holds different viewpoints from those of his own parents. If your family always gathers at the table for meals, he may be initially uncomfortable with a family that eats on the run. He may come home and report that his friend's family does things "wrong." By six, however, he may question why he can't eat his dinner on the floor while drawing just as his friend does rather than sitting at the table as he's expected to do with you.

Your child's temperament will, in many ways, affect how he handles the differences between your house rules and the rules at friends' homes. An easy child will take great pains to abide by the rules that are set forth no matter where he is. A more challenging child might respond differently. If, for example, you allow your child to wear his shoes in the house and if his playmate's mom mentions that the rule in their house is to remove shoes at the door, he may respond, "No, I'm allowed to keep my shoes on." He may become very upset if the other mom insists that he remove his shoes. He's not intentionally being defiant. In his view, he's simply letting the other mom know that he has different rules.

As your child increasingly joins social situations that are outside the reach of your authority, it becomes important to let him know that he's expected to comply with another family's rules when he is at their home or going out with them as long as those rules don't make him uncomfortable or feel wrong to him. You may want to give examples, such as "If Jason's mom says, 'Don't eat any of the cookies before dinner,' then you should obey. But if she says, 'You don't have to use a helmet when you ride your bike,' you should say, 'I'm not allowed to ride unless I wear a helmet.'" Let him know, too, that his friends make similar adjustments in your home. Get in the habit of announcing a rule or two when playmates visit your child at your house. Saying something such as "Our house rule is that we don't play games in the living room" helps your child as well as the visitor understand that families, while sharing certain rules, differ on others.

## CONFLICT
# Living up to rising expectations

Your child's desire to please you is always his biggest motivation to behave. Right now particularly, he'll do whatever he can to show you how cooperative he can be. Trouble can arise, however, from his recognition—and yours—that the expectations for his behavior are becoming greater than they once were.

Only last year, you seemed to allow far more leeway. You didn't expect too much in the way of responsibility or self-discipline and he had learned to negotiate a safe path through a very wide field of acceptable behavior. Now the field is narrowing, and he's bumping into new constraints every day. The rules, clearly, are changing faster than his maturity can keep up with. With more opportunities for conflict, your child slips into behaviors that are now misbehaviors.

Perhaps last year, you were able to allow him plenty of time to unwind at the end of the day. Now, he may have homework to do, and he needs to be more organized than is natural for him. You tell him to hurry up, to keep his papers neat, to skip some playtime to devote to reading. His response may be to dawdle. Or he may whine. Or maybe he'll just refuse to cooperate. Or out of frustration and clumsiness, he may spill a glass of milk all over his uncompleted work, creating a distraction from the things he finds difficult or unpleasant. In some ways, his behavior mimics that of a toddler, but now you have less patience for it. And because he's grown into such a big, capable kid, you're less likely to excuse his immaturity and more likely to view these misbehaviors as defiance.

It's not that your child doesn't have higher expectations for himself as well. Like you and his teachers, he believes he's capable of being good all (or, at least, most) of the time, and he badly wants to live up to that ideal. But he simply can't. As he begins to think of himself in less than glowing terms, he may even conclude that he's bad. From there, he begins to experiment with behavior that he associates with being bad. "I'm no good at sitting still like I'm supposed to" becomes "I'm no good." For most kids, this bleak self-evaluation passes quickly. But if you get too caught up in correcting him for misbehaviors without balancing that with praise for good behavior, your child's sense of himself as bad will take root. Then, his behavior will be much more difficult for you to manage and for him to manage himself.

## YOU AND YOUR CHILD
## Encouraging positive behavior
Much of what adults call "misbehavior" is really a mismatch between expectations and reality. Knowing what your child is really capable of, knowing his need to show off being good, and adjusting your responses to him can change your relationship from one fraught with conflict to one of mutual understanding. To help your child behave in a way that will make him want to continue behaving well:

*Be realistic about his limitations.* Don't ask your five- or six-year-old to be polite to company for hours on end. After the introductions, let him go off and play until it's dinnertime. And then don't ask that he sit through any lengthy adult conversation. Small practice sessions in acquiring mature social skills will result in the appearance of consistently good manners far more than trying to force the issue just yet. At dinner, don't overload his plate. Being overwhelmed by more than he wants or can comfortably finish is a setup for conflict. Even though he's capable of cleaning up after himself in individual bits, don't expect him to keep his room in order on his own. Practice a one-thing-at-a-time approach until he's ready—a few years from now—to take on an entire job himself. In the meantime, involve him in straightening his room with steps such as "Let's make the bed." When that's done, move on to "Put the books on the shelf," and so on.

***Give your child opportunities to show off.*** How much of your child's "misbehavior" is really just the result of his wanting to show off his latest accomplishment at an inconvenient time? You get angry when he interrupts a phone call or when he can't settle down to practice writing numbers. Instead, he wants to show you how he's learned to hop on one foot or to cross his eyes, just like a cool kid at school. Realize that over the course of the day, your child is anxious to impress you, and give him lots of chances to do so. Before making a phone call, for instance, say, "Show me that new trick you learned." After he has done so, praise him, and tell him that you now need a few minutes to talk on the phone.

***Maintain a predictable routine.*** Well-established routines help all kids get through the day with less fuss, but to a five- or six-year-old who has entered a whole new world of school, a routine is a safety net like no other. The routine doesn't have to be so rigid that it doesn't allow for spontaneity, but the major parts of the day—getting up and out, returning from school, doing homework, having dinner, and going to bed—should follow a predictable pattern. Enhance the weekly routine by planning fun activities too—such as Wednesday night pizza dinner or Thursday night game night, so that the idea as well as the practice of the routine is something to anticipate happily.

*Find things to praise.* Catch your child doing something right. When you notice that he tied his own shoe without asking for help, simply say, "That was great how you tied your shoe by yourself." When he shares a cookie with his younger sibling, pat his head and say, "I'm proud to see you sharing so well." Let him know every day that he's done something well, even if it's a bit of a stretch on a bad day.

*Provide outlets to deal with any frustrations.* Make sure that your child has down time in which nothing much is expected of him. Let him laze in front of the TV for half an hour. Leave him alone while he works on an art or building project that interests him. Don't correct him if he's biting his nails or tapping his pencil while he works. Having to concentrate on the work at hand and on preventing soothing behaviors at the same time can simply be too difficult to handle.

*Make sure he is well nourished and rested.* Lack of wholesome foods and too little sleep can lead even the most mild-tempered child into trouble.

*Offer rewards for growing up.* At this stage in his life, your child may begin to wonder if growing up and being responsible is really such a great thing after all. He may feel burdened by the new demands and not see a counterpoint in expanded privileges. Make a point of letting him know that he's earned the privilege of staying up a half hour later, or of getting to choose his own backpack now that he's bigger.

*Prepare ahead.* Sometimes, misbehavior is really just a matter of not knowing what to do and what is acceptable. Before placing your child in a new situation, lay out the ground rules. Explain what is likely to happen at an event or occasion and let him know how he's expected to behave.

## Common misbehaviors and how to deal with them

Despite your and your child's best efforts, he will sometimes do things that need your correction. At this age, the list of common misbehaviors is blessedly short:

*Aggression.* While your five- or six-year-old is far less likely than a toddler to bite or pinch a playmate, he may not have given up on all his aggressive impulses yet. Hitting, pushing, and shoving, while less common at this age, can occur when a child feels physically or emotionally threatened. It's imperative that you respond immediately to acts of aggression, but not with physical punishment; this only serves to undermine your lesson about not resorting to hitting. Firmly talk to your child about what else he could have done rather than attempting to hurt a playmate. Could he have explained his feelings in words instead? Could he have simply walked away? Recognize his anger, especially if it is justified, but explain that he cannot resort to violence. If he feels he must hit in self-defense, teach him the better alternative of alerting an adult to deal with an aggressor. If impatience is the cause of pushing or shoving another child, work with your child to develop patience. You can drive the lesson home by requiring your child to wait out a desired activity as a result of his aggression. Make a point of showing empathy for the victim, and have your child think of ways to negotiate peace with whomever he has fought. Most often, physical fighting among five- and six-year-olds is a result of frustration and immaturity. If, however, your child regularly gets involved in physical altercations, talk to the school guidance counselor or your child's physician to find out where to get appropriate professional help.

*Dawdling.* Stretching out the time needed to complete a task is often a child's way of saying, "I can't do it all." This is his nonverbal way of expressing frustration about being asked to "keep up"— with his schedule, with you, and with all the expectations everyone has for him. If dawdling happens more than occasionally, look for ways to reduce stress in your child's life. Give him more time in the morning to get ready for school, or more unstructured time in the afternoon so that he feels less pressure overall. He'll be very responsive to games to get him moving. A playful challenge, such as "Let's see if you can get ready before this song is finished on the radio," might be all you need to speed him up. Rewards are also effective: "When you finish picking up your toys, I'll read to you."

*Whining.* Whining is a learned behavior, and if your child is whining at the age of five or six, he's learned that it can be an effective way to get what he wants. Usually, what he really wants is your attention. The more you offer your attention for positive actions, the less he'll feel compelled to whine to get you to take notice. If your child does whine, ignore it if you can. Simply say, "I can't respond to you when you use that voice." And then don't. Your child will make a noble attempt to revert to big-kid talking when he sees that whining doesn't work.

*Fibbing.* At five, your child is not entirely clear on the difference between real and make-believe. He believes that if he says something, then it can be true. At six, he understands a little better, but he will still lie if he thinks it will get him out of trouble. At either age, if he knocks over your favorite lamp while playing basketball in the living room, he'll likely deny his role in the disaster. To help your child not paint himself into a lie that he feels he must defend, learn to phrase your questions in a manner that will elicit the truth. For example, asking "Did you knock over the lamp?" will more than likely result in a "No, not me." Asking "How did you think I'd feel when I saw that you broke the lamp?" however, gets your child past the denial and into an apology.

*Stealing.* Most five- to six-year-olds have at least one experience with larceny. A usual reaction—hiding or breaking the pilfered object—points to their growing ability to feel bad about doing something wrong. If your child takes something that doesn't belong to him, don't overreact. Explain why it is wrong to take what doesn't belong to him. Help him make amends, either by returning the stolen object to its rightful owner or, if he's lost or damaged it, to replace it. Do not apply a harsh label, such as calling your child a thief. He'll think of himself that way, which could lead to more of the same behavior rather than eliminating it.

## HELPING YOUR CHILD GROW
## Useful responses to misbehavior

It's important to differentiate between nonnegotiable rules and those that have a little wiggle room. You need to be firm and consistent with safety and morality issues, but other rules might be a bit more flexible. For instance, your child needs to learn that he can never ride his bike without his helmet and that he cannot, under any circumstances, injure another person. But perhaps he could watch an extra half hour of TV on a school night sometimes.

While some circumstances call for very specific responses— such as helping your child return something to its owner if he took it—many common misbehaviors can be handled in more wide-ranging ways:

***Ignore it.*** While you don't want to give your child the sense that anything goes, sometimes looking the other way when your child has committed a small infraction is best for everyone. Being scrutinized all the time and feeling that a mistake or a brief outburst must be met with a correction can cause great stress. Ignoring a small misbehavior, such as when your child doesn't put his toys away when he's done playing even though he's supposed to, won't ruin him and will help to make him more aware of the difference between the nonnegotiable rules and those that are less important.

***Offer him another chance.*** Imagine your child's relief when he's realized he's being really disobedient and you offer him a reprieve.

If your child is defiant or badly dawdling, don't correct him immediately. Instead, say something like, "I think you'll need three chances to do the right thing this time." This gives your child a chance to rethink his stance and to comply without losing face.

*Negotiate.* This is not the same as bribing. With a bribe your child basically gets something for doing what's expected of him. Negotiation recognizes his needs as well as your own and seeks to find a way of making compliance a win-win situation. Say, for instance, your child dislikes having his hair washed. Before beginning, ask him if he'd rather have an extra bedtime story or a special treat after the hair washing. This acknowledges that you're respecting his feelings by offering to tip the balance of activities back in his favor in exchange for his cooperation. And once in a while, simply give in when your child makes a good argument for wanting or not wanting to do something of little consequence.

*Use logical consequences.* Connect the "crime" to the punishment in a logical way. If your child rides his bike without putting on his helmet, take away his bike for a few days. If he makes a mess, have him work on the cleanup. If he misbehaves at the playground after receiving a warning, take him home.

*Change your approach.* If you correct your child with an overused phrase such as "That's not nice!" he may tune you out. If, however, you toss a big word at him, saying, for instance, "That is totally unacceptable!" he'll stop and take notice. He's not crazy about being corrected, but he is glad to hear you speak to him with new and interesting vocabulary.

*Stick to the issue at hand.* Deal with one issue at a time when addressing a misbehavior. Don't bring up past misbehaviors or attach any kind of demeaning label to your child, such as "brat" or "liar."

## Handling your own anger

It can be difficult to accept how the child you love so much can bring out such intense feelings of anger sometimes. It's important to accept that children can, indeed, trigger feelings of rage. Giving in to that rage by screaming or striking out at your child, however, only undermines your own self-esteem and your ability to discipline effectively. When their parents respond to them in angry, hurtful ways, children soon learn to ignore the outburst or to simply try to stay out of their parents' way. Some may appear compliant in the face of such anger, but they're concerned more with how not to get caught misbehaving rather than trying to correct their own behavior. Let's face it: A child whose parents are out of control is not thinking about self-improvement. He's far more concerned with weathering the storm.

If your relationship is generally loving and strong, an occasional blowup won't change that. And trying to keep your anger buried won't help you or your child. The best way to deal with the anger that is a natural part of a strong relationship is to acknowledge it and to let your child know that his behavior has caused you to feel angry. Your child feels anger too sometimes, and he needs reassurances that it can be a healthy and normal response to a situation. He also needs to see that talking about and trying to correct the events that lead to anger are appropriate ways of dealing with this strong emotion.

If you find yourself feeling a surge of anger at your child, stop for a moment and try to remember that he's not aiming to make you angry—even if he's being defiant. He wants to please you. Try to rephrase your thinking from "He's driving me crazy with his dawdling" to "He needs more time to get ready," which is a much less explosive explanation. If you do lash out and say unfair or hurtful things, apologize. Let your child know that you recognize your own misbehavior. Explain what made you angry and tell him how you will handle your feelings the next time. Reassure him that even though his behavior upset you, you still love him completely. It is also a good lesson for your child to learn that anger isn't a permanent state—a person can recover from it.

# That's not fair!

## Your child's moral development

"That's not fair!" could easily be the motto of your kindergarten or first-grade child. Between the ages of five and six, your child is deeply concerned about issues of fairness and right and wrong. After all, she's putting an enormous amount of energy into "being good," and she wants everyone else to be good, too.

Ironically, her need to demonstrate being good can, because of your child's immaturity, cause her to fib or even steal to assure herself of her goodness. As discussed in the previous chapter, she might deny responsibility for an action because she believes that a "good" child could not have accidentally broken her sister's favorite bracelet. By saying "I didn't do it," she's trying to spare herself the bad feelings that come from doing something she wished she hadn't. She might take a soccer ball that belongs to a good soccer player, reasoning that "I can be a good player too, if I take her ball." Then, she might hide or destroy the ball as a way of redeeming herself. "If I make it go away, then I didn't really take it."

Your child's immaturity and lack of experience can cause her a great deal of confusion about what's right and what's wrong, what's expected of her, and what response she's supposed to have to her own and to others' behavior. A typical five-year-old is something of a "kindergarten cop," always on the lookout for others' misdeeds. She may become, for a time, quite a "tattler" in her effort to help her peers follow the straight and narrow path that she is trying so hard to follow herself. If her classmate draws a purple elephant, your child may feel compelled to inform the teacher that so-and-so isn't following the "rules" about elephant colors.

The rightness and wrongness she observes doesn't necessarily have anything to do with morality. Rule following is separate at this stage from true matters of conscience. Increasingly, however, as your child approaches age seven, she will form a better understanding of right and wrong. By age six, she may understand that, though elephants really aren't purple, there's nothing fundamentally wrong with choosing a purple crayon to draw one. Now she may start to consider the same issues that adults do: It's wrong to hurt others. It's right to be helpful. It's wrong to take something that's not yours. It's right to tell the truth. Your six-year-old may not always abide by these standards, but she is beginning to internalize them.

## DEVELOPMENTAL MILESTONE
### An internal sense of right and wrong

Until recently, your child's sense of right and wrong consisted solely of what you would and wouldn't let her do. By the age of three or four, your child understood some of your expectations: sharing her toys, taking turns, refraining from hitting. Now she knows it's wrong to hit someone even if you're not watching. (But she still feels far worse about hitting another if she's caught.)

Like the process of becoming intellectually mature, the development of your child's conscience is a gradual process. One day, she knows the difference between real and imaginary. The next day (or even the next minute), she's caught up in a fantasy that seems very real to her. Similarly, one moment she knows right from wrong, but the next, she's a bit fuzzy on it.

As with all things, she's looking to you for guidance: She wants you to explain to her why certain behaviors are preferable to others. Her growing intellectual skills, however, won't allow her to accept your words if they aren't reflected by your actions. Hypocrisy in adult actions can seriously undermine your child's entry into a mature morality.

## Teaching your child values

Your values are the rules you choose to live by, not the rules you talk about. More than ever before, your child is watching you and learning. She's paying attention to what you say—but even more, to what you do. If you tell her to "be nice," but are then rude to a school employee, what she's learned is that "being nice" is really optional, or perhaps that it is something that children must do, but from which grown-ups are exempt. That's confusing to a child at any age, but especially to a five- or six-year-old who is proudly demonstrating her own goodness.

Teaching your child values permeates everything you do together. Your open and friendly gestures to the neighbors, something as simple as a daily wave across the street to say "Good morning," shows your child that neighborliness is good. Were you to walk outdoors in the morning and kick over the neighbor's garbage can because it encroached on your property, your child would learn to value her own property over that of the neighbor's and that it is acceptable to show displeasure by damaging another's property. Alerting a store clerk that she gave you too much change teaches your child the importance of honesty. On the other hand, if you were to confide in your child that this was your lucky day because the clerk accidentally gave you an extra ten dollars, you would be teaching her that it's a good thing to benefit from another's error and that taking what's not yours from a store is okay as long as you don't get caught.

Now, your child is better equipped to understand the reasons behind your insistence on certain behaviors. At the most primitive level, she's learning that certain behaviors are unacceptable because they ultimately impinge on her own self-interests. "If I toss sand in the sandbox, other children won't want to play with me." This form of knowing "right" from "wrong" is not morality, but it can help a child judge for herself if an action is good or bad, and to internalize the rule. Your child takes a leap into a more mature sense of right and wrong when she develops empathy, the ability to imagine herself in another person's position.

## Raising an empathetic child

Most likely, you planted the seeds of empathy when your child was quite young and you responded to a misbehavior with a statement such as "How do you think it makes your friend feel when you toss sand at him?" Your child's ability to recognize that someone else has feelings and rights like her own is a major step in development.

Empathy permeates almost all issues of morality, both in preventing your child from acting unkindly toward another and in helping her decide to put aside her own needs for the good of others. Since children can't always see the potential victim of a misbehavior, however, they need caring adults to point out the "why" of positive behavior.

In the example of getting too much change at the store, your child may not understand why you should return the money you received in error. She may see a cash register full of bills and conclude that the store won't miss what you've received. But you can explain that the clerk may have to pay back the missing money at the end of the workday. Or the store may lose some of the money it earned.

Empathy, of course, is more than a motivation to avoid doing wrong. It is also an imperative to do right. When you help your child buy a toy for a holiday toy drive for needy children, you are giving her the gift of seeing her power to change the world for the better. When riding a public bus, a sense of empathy can help your child graciously give up her seat to another rider. To help your child understand why it's good to offer her seat, talk to her about it in a matter-of-fact way before boarding the bus, just as you might talk to her about stopping at the corner to look both ways before crossing the street when you're taking a walk. Explain that when the bus is crowded there may not be enough seats for all the passengers and that if she sees an older or disabled person standing, she can do a good deed by moving from a seat onto your lap. She may, of course, give up the seat if you simply say, "Sit on my lap, so this lady can have your seat," but her pleasure in doing it won't be the same as it will be when she understands that she is giving a gift to someone whose need for the seat is greater than her own.

In order to feel empathy, your child needs to experience receiving empathy. Asking for blind obedience, even when she's tired or had a bad day, doesn't allow her to see empathy at work. But when you say, "I know you're too tired to clean up your room today, so let's just leave the toys on the floor until tomorrow," you inform your child that you've taken her position and showed an understanding of what it means to be her right now. When you apologize after an angry outburst, your child has another example of being the beneficiary of empathy. Learning to put herself in another's position doesn't come all at once, and few children (or adults) act with empathy on all occasions. But a habit of looking to see the world from another's perspective can become part of your child's character if she's given the opportunity to practice kindness on a regular basis.

**Helping your child evaluate situations from a moral angle**

Few parents would ever say to a child that lying is good. Yet few would congratulate their child for blurting out, "This pie is disgusting," after taking a bite of dessert that a guest has brought to the house. Teaching children the moral value of honesty along with the social value of discretion is no easy task.

As your child enters her early school years, she will increasingly be faced with seemingly conflicting moral choices. For example, she may have learned the social skill "It's not nice to tattle." She also may have been taught that it's important to be loyal to a friend, and to keep a secret if a friend has asked her to. On another occasion, she learned that she should tell a grown-up if something's troubling her. What should she do, then, if a friend confides that she has a backpack full of firecrackers and a book of matches? Should she tell a grown-up? Or is that tattling? Is she being disloyal if she tells a secret?

Since you can't possibly anticipate all the circumstances that your child might encounter, your best means of clarifying your values are to offer contingencies along with rules and to communicate about moral values on a regular basis. Underline your messages with information about how your child's actions need to begin from a basis of empathy.

In the instance of the bad-tasting pie, you do not want your child to smile and say "Mmm, good" if that's not true. Neither do you want her to go on about how bad it is. If such an incident took place in front of the baker, simply correct your child with a short "Even if you don't like it, it's not polite to say that it's disgusting." Later, talk to her about the pie-giver's feelings. Help her think of other truthful things she could say that would not be hurtful, such as "It's not my favorite kind of pie" or simply "No thank you." In the case of tattling versus telling a grown-up about a potentially dangerous activity, explain that some rules are more important than others. Say something like, "Tattling isn't always good and keeping a secret sometimes can be good, but you would be doing your friend a favor if you tell a grown-up that she could do something to hurt herself or someone else." Since that's a lot for a young child to grasp, create a number of scenarios to bring the lesson home: "What would you do if your friend wanted to throw water balloons from the school bathroom onto the playground below?" for example.

### The truth about honesty

Children lie for the same reasons grown-ups do—to avoid getting into trouble or to avoid living up to their responsibilities. Your child might tell you that she's finished with her homework when she hasn't, because she knows she can't watch TV until her homework is done. To help your child tell the truth, you need to help her understand the reasons why honesty really is the best policy.

Explain that your ability to trust her word is one of the foundations of your relationship. Ask your child what she thinks things would be like between the two of you if you could not believe what she tells you. Ask her how she would feel about you if you didn't tell her the truth. Of course, you need to be truthful with her, too, even when it's inconvenient. For instance, if you say, "I'll take you to the park after dinner," but then don't follow through because something else has come up, your child will learn not to trust your word. (If such an event is extremely rare, however, you can help your child understand that you're sorry that you weren't able to keep your word.) If you regularly break promises, your child's trust in you and your word will be greatly diminished.

### CONFLICT
## Why isn't everything perfect?

Between the ages of five and seven, your child is learning that a larger world than she has imagined exists, and that in that world, bad things can happen. She may have caught glimpses on the evening news of natural disasters or crimes that injured or killed innocent people. Closer to home, she may have a friend who has experienced a great loss in her family or she may have experienced a loss herself.

Because five- and six-year-olds are still amazingly self-centered, your child may feel responsible for bad things that take place near home. If a friend is very ill, for instance, your child may worry that the friend is sick because she was unkind to him at recess. If you and your spouse are divorcing, she may feel it's because she hasn't been good. For distant hurts that she hears about, she may become troubled about her inability to make everything okay. She also may feel vulnerable. If bad things can happen to others, is she safe?

Feeling both so powerful and so ineffectual simultaneously is quite troubling. Your child may look for someone else to blame so that she doesn't have to continue feeling responsible. She may blame you. Many children ask, "How can God let this happen?" when they witness or hear about dreadful things. For your five- or six-year-old, your answer to this question needs to support her hope that neither she, nor you, nor God is responsible for bad things happening. You can explain that everyone, perhaps even God, is very sad when people get hurt.

Because rules have taken on such meaning for your child, she may question why rules aren't changed so that bad things don't happen. For example, when she learns that some people live in poverty, she might want to know why all the money in the world isn't divided equally among all people so that no one has to do without.

It's important to give your child opportunities to right some of the wrongs she sees in the world. Encourage her to contribute some of the money she received for her birthday to a relief organization. Help her sort her outgrown clothes and toys to contribute them to children whose parents can't afford new items. Help her write and send cards to people who are not feeling well. Knowing that she can help alleviate some of the troubles in the world can help her realign her good feelings about herself with her need to know that the world is basically a good place. But be very careful not to make your child feel that the world's problems are hers to solve. Reassure her that grown-ups are working hard to make things better and that her role is to handle the job of being a kid.

## YOU AND YOUR CHILD
# Helping your child develop personal values

Your child's values will evolve over her lifetime. To get her started on the right track:

*Model appropriate behavior.* Your actions speak far louder than your words.

*Discuss your values.* Tell your child why you act the way you do. As you're sending a check to a charity, say, "I think it's important for us to help others who have less than we do." Even for something as simple as waiting for the light to change rather than crossing against the red, say, "If I step out now, a driver would not expect me. I could get hurt and I could also cause someone else to get hurt."

*Point out examples of good and bad behavior.* Point out instances of moral behavior when you encounter it: "Isn't that nice how that girl is helping the older man carry his groceries." If a television show features a character getting what she wants through deceit or violence, talk to your child about better ways the character could have behaved.

*Compliment your child for good choices.* When you've observed your child engaged in an act of kindness, such as sharing a cookie, make a note of it.

*Talk about people whose character you admire.* Let your child know what personal traits are admirable: "I like Mr. Smith because he's always willing to help out the neighbors," or "I admire Sarah because she works so hard to keep up with her schoolwork. She doesn't give up."

***Explain the reason for your rules.*** Having rules for rules' sake doesn't teach any lessons about right and wrong. Explaining that your child isn't allowed to use racial slurs because it's hurtful and because such language limits her and another person's opportunity to get to know one another is more effective than simply saying, "That's not nice."

***Monitor the media.*** Don't be afraid to limit your child's involvement in media that you find morally offensive. Take a stand, saying, "You're not allowed to see that movie with your friends because I think it's too violent and it shows people handling their problems in the wrong way." Be sure to provide opportunities, however, for your child to enjoy appropriate entertainment.

***Talk about your own moral struggles.*** Don't be afraid to let your child see you deal with moral quandaries and to let her know that sometimes there are no easy answers.

| If your child... | Do say | Don't say |
| --- | --- | --- |
| excludes a playmate from a game | "How would you feel if you were left out?" | "You're so mean." |
| tells a fib | "It's important for me to be able to trust you." | "I don't like liars." |
| purposely breaks a sibling's toy | "You'll have to replace it." And give her an opportunity to do so. | "Now your brother can break your toy." |

## HELPING YOUR CHILD GROW
# Helping your child learn from her mistakes

In the course of developing and learning to live by a moral code, your child will make some mistakes. Punitive responses do little at this stage to help a child develop a sense of morality, which is your goal now. When your child has misbehaved in a manner that goes against your moral code:

*Discuss why the behavior is unacceptable.* Emphasize how her actions affect others as well as herself.

*Don't be afraid to make her feel a bit guilty.* Guilt can be a great motivator since no one, especially a five- or six-year-old, likes to feel bad about herself. Don't overdo it though, since an overwhelming feeling of shame can make your child feel incapable of doing good.

*Never label a child by her mistake.* Calling her a "bad girl" or a "thief" makes her think of herself in those terms rather than as a person who's capable of redeeming herself. Focus on her actions, saying, for instance, "I don't like what you did. You shouldn't take something that isn't yours." Such a statement lets your child know that it's her behavior, not her whole being, that needs to change.

*Give your child the chance to take responsibility for her actions.* Teach her to speak in the active voice, saying, for instance, "I broke the bracelet" rather than "It broke."

*Most important, help her find ways to make amends.* If she's been hurtful to a friend, help her think of ways to apologize. If she's taken something that isn't hers, help her to return it.

## The importance of manners

Manners are more than social niceties. They represent a level of respect for others and as such are an important part of your child's moral development. Teaching your child both the "rules" of manners as well as the meaning behind these rules and relating them to events in your child's life will make your lessons much more meaningful. Now, your child is ready to learn manners such as:

*Being quiet at certain times.* In places such as theaters, places of worship, and classrooms, explain that other people can't hear what's being said and their pleasure, thoughts, and learning are interrupted by unnecessary talking. Ask how your child would feel if everyone talked during her favorite TV program. Would she be able to enjoy it? Would she be able to concentrate?

*Holding doors for others.* By holding the door, you're saying, "I notice you and I'd like to take this chance to help you." Help your child see that by holding the door, she makes another person feel good, much as she feels good when someone does something nice for her. Letting a door go, on the other hand, risks injuring another.

*Not interrupting.* Conversations are about talking *and* listening. How does your child feel when she's unable to finish what she's saying? What if no one bothered to listen? Explain that everyone feels upset when they aren't allowed to finish talking.

*Greeting people politely.* Saying hello to others in a gracious way is a means of acknowledging that person. Ask your child how she would feel if she were ignored. Let her know that she's now old enough not to hide behind you or otherwise be exempt from taking part in the exchange of greetings.

# Keep me safe

## Helping your child avoid harm

In many ways, you can breathe a sigh of relief when your child turns five. Far less impulsive and with more skills than ever before, your child can—finally—be out of your line of vision for minutes at a time at home without requiring you to hop up and make sure that he's safe. Added to that, he's developed a sense of caution. He's more likely to evaluate a situation before plunging into it. Because he's so good at so much, he may not feel that he has to try things that even he deems outside his expertise.

Your child's growing competence, however, shouldn't lull you into the sense that you can forgo your vigilance entirely. His new skills and your newfound confidence still can lead him into new dangers. It remains as important as ever to review your child's surroundings for hazards. Although you no longer have to make sure that access to the stairs is blocked, you now need to make sure that he doesn't try to use kitchen appliances himself. You may be able to leave him unsupervised in his room, but he needs the same level of watching when you're at the mall. So it isn't really fewer concerns you'll have now, just different ones.

## DEVELOPMENTAL MILESTONE
### Caution

Your child's trepidation when he approaches certain activities now seems to contradict his generally enthusiastic nature. How can this child, who runs, skips, and jumps down the sidewalk, hold on to you so tightly when he's learning to ride a two-wheeler? Is it the same child who happily turns the hose on his playmates who now clings to the side of the pool? There's really no contradiction. Your child is simply looking to balance his continued development in some areas with a need to hold off and even retreat from other forms of development.

If your child is naturally timid and slow to warm up, he'll be even more so when it comes to trying out new skills. If he's generally active, you may notice him slowing down a bit or focusing his energies on just a few skills that he's determined to improve.

## CONFLICT
### Advance and Retreat

It's a big world out there, and your child is anxious to take his place in it. On the other hand, it's a big world out there, and your child is just plain anxious. He's now more aware that unintended and terrible things can happen. After overhearing a news report about an earthquake on the other side of the world, you may find him insisting that you explain again and again how *your* house is built on a solid foundation and that he's safe.

Upon entering school, where larger classes and less playground supervision are the rule, he may find that a schoolyard bully has picked him out. How does he handle a real threat? He knows he's not supposed to fight, but what about defending himself? Can he still, now that he's a big kid, go to you or to his teacher for protection? New sports and other activities beckon, and he may find himself with more skinned knees than he bargained for. He's concerned about the impression he's making on his peers; if he cries, will they call him names? Emotionally, he may feel somewhat alone these days as he tries mightily to wear the stoic mask of a big kid while feeling very vulnerable inside.

As he edges toward six and into age seven, your child will regain his equilibrium. His sense of safety will likely be stronger as his experiences teach him that, yes, indeed, the world is safe enough to venture into and his place in it is secure.

Your child's worries during this phase of his life tend to center around things he's just recently learned about or is experiencing for the very first time—a mixture of the fantastic and the mundane: Will he remember to get off the school bus at the right stop? Will aliens take over the planet? Will he wet his pants or otherwise embarrass himself among his new schoolmates? Could violence rock his school?

It's important to recognize and respect your child's fears and to assure him that you and other grown-ups are taking care of him. It's also important to be on the alert for the things that really do pose a danger to your child. According to the National Safe Kids Campaign, the most likely causes of death and injury to five- and six-year-olds are car and pedestrian accidents, followed by drowning and near-drowning incidents, fires and burns, and playground accidents. Other preventable causes of harm include schoolbus incidents, at-home accidents, and firearms. Following are ways you can work with your child to keep him safe:

## Car and pedestrian accidents

Car accidents account for more than 40 percent of all childhood injuries and fatalities. Most serious harm could be prevented by the use of proper restraints and proper positioning of your child within the vehicle. When your child outgrows the car seat that was designed to keep a child under 40 pounds safe, it's tempting to think that a seat belt alone could keep your five- or six-year-old secure in case of a car accident. But kids between 40 and 75 pounds and under 58 inches tall are simply too small to be protected adequately by a seat belt. The use of a booster seat designed for children through age 9 or 75 lbs. when used with a seat belt, however, could drastically reduce injuries and deaths.

Children under the age of 12 should also ride in the backseat of a car or the middle seat of a three-row van. If the vehicle has side airbags, seat your child in the middle of the seat, or disable the airbags. Children under 12 or under 58 inches should never sit in the front seat of a car.

Never leave a child alone in a car, even for a minute. Active five- and six-year-olds have been known to play with the gears and can accidentally release the brakes. Though carjackings are rare, leaving your child in a running vehicle for even a few seconds puts him at risk. And when the temperature is above 80 degrees Fahrenheit, the temperature inside the car could reach over 100 degrees in just minutes, and a child left sleeping in a car could suffer heatstroke, brain damage, and even death.

As a pedestrian, your five- or six-year-old is more at risk than an older child or an adult due partly to his impulsivity, and partly because he's just too small for drivers to see him. While he may no longer need to hold your hand at each crossing, he does need to stay immediately next to you. This is also true in parking lots, where young children are particularly vulnerable.

Teach your child to stop completely before stepping off the curb or before crossing a driveway. He should look both ways and always follow the light, if there is one. And he should never enter the street from between parked cars or dart between cars in a parking lot. Five- and six-year-olds, even though they can repeat the rules of street crossing to you and demonstrate their understanding when they're with you, are not consistently mature enough to be allowed to cross the street on their own. That ability doesn't usually come until a child is about eight years old.

## A note about schoolbus safety

Schoolbuses, while not perfect, are a relatively safe means of transportation. The majority of injuries associated with schoolbuses take place outside the vehicle. It's vital to teach your child these rules about staying safe while boarding and getting off a schoolbus:

- **Never run or walk alongside the bus.** The driver cannot see a child who's positioned against the outer wall of the bus. Most schoolbus deaths and injuries occur when a child is too close to the bus and is hit by the back wheels, knocking him under when the bus moves.
- **Never walk closely in front of the bus.** From his or her perch in the driver's seat, the driver cannot see a child who's less than four feet from the front of the bus.
- **Never try to retrieve anything that has fallen near the bus.** Teach your child to alert a parent or the driver if something has fallen within a danger zone around the bus.
- **Wear snug-fitting clothing and backpacks.** Clothing and supplies can get caught in bus fenders or doors. Long straps hanging from backpacks can get caught in closing doors and the bus driver may not notice that a child is being dragged.
- **Behave.** Bus drivers need to pay attention to the road, not to misbehaving children. Teach your child to obey all safety rules presented by his driver, including to remain seated for the entire ride, never to put his hands or head out the window, and never to toss anything from the window.

**Drowning**

Most drownings and near-drownings occur in home swimming pools, though hot tubs, spa baths, and natural bodies of water also pose a real risk to children under the age of 14.

The keys to preventing these tragedies are placing adequate barriers around pools and hot tubs; closely supervising your child when he's around water, including baths (especially spa jets); and being prepared in case of an emergency. All parents, but especially those who have home pools, should be trained in child CPR.

All at-home, in-ground pools should be surrounded by fencing that is at least four feet high or by a safety cover. Ladders should be removed from aboveground pools when they are not in use. A phone should always be close by to call for help and to keep adults from leaving the poolside to answer calls. Children should never be allowed to swim without a competent adult present. Flotation devices are never a substitute for constant supervision.

While five- and six-year-olds are capable of learning to swim, their abilities should not be seen as protection against drowning. Even the best swimmers can become panicky, receive a head injury, or otherwise be prevented from using their skills.

The profusion of home spas and hot tubs has increased the level of risk for drowning in the home. Hot tubs are not recommended for children under age 10 or under 90 pounds, even with supervision. The water temperature can raise a child's temperature to dangerous levels. (Adults, too, should limit their time in hot tubs and keep the water temperature no higher than 104 degrees Fahrenheit to avoid heat-related illness.) Children should never, ever be allowed to put their heads underwater in home spas or baths that contain suction jets and/or high-suction drains since hair and/or limbs can become entrapped underwater.

When on a boat or near a dock, your child should always wear a Coast Guard–approved life vest that is designed to keep his head above water even if he's unconscious. Children should avoid going more than calf-deep in waves at ocean beaches where they could be knocked down and swept away by the undertow. Parents or other responsible adults should hold kids' hands as they play near a rough tide.

## Fire

Fires and burns are the third leading cause of injury and death in kids under the age of 14. Most fire-related deaths and injuries occur at home, especially in homes that do not have working smoke detectors. It is absolutely essential that your home have at least one alarm on each level of the home and that you change the batteries regularly—twice a year. A good way to remember is to change the batteries when the clocks are set back and ahead in fall and spring. A significant portion of fire deaths and injuries are the result of children, especially four- and five-year-olds, playing with matches or lighters.

By the age of five, your child is ready for significant fire-safety instruction. Now is the time to teach your child:

*Never play with matches or lighters.* Train your child to alert you to any matchbooks or lighters he finds in the house. Remind him that it's never "tattling" to tell you about another child who has access to fire-starting materials.

*Stop, drop, and roll.* In panic, a child whose clothing catches fire often runs for help, which only fans the flames. Teach your child to stop where he is, drop to the ground, and roll around and around to put out the flames. If his sleeves are on fire, he should keep his arms at his sides. If his sleeves are not on fire, he should cover his face while he rolls.

*Know the sound of the smoke detector and what it means.* Demonstrate the sound that your smoke detector makes and tell your child that if he ever hears this sound, he's to alert you immediately if he can and get out of the house if he sees or smells smoke.

**Get out.** Young children often hide under a bed or in a closet when faced with a fire. Teach your child that the safest place for him to be is outside. If your child sleeps in an upper-story room, equip the room with a window ladder fire escape and show your child how to use it. Equip the ladder with an alarm so you'll be alerted to its use—during an emergency, or no emergency. Be sure to warn your child that the ladder will make a loud noise when used so that the alarm does not frighten him in the event of a fire emergency.

**Get low and go.** Smoke filling a room rises, so the air near the floor is less smoky. If your child is ever in a smoke-filled room, teach him to crawl along the floor to an exit.

**Know your way out.** Teach your child the best way to exit your home in the event of a fire, as well as a secondary escape route if the main exit is impassable. Predesignate a place to meet outside.

**Touch a door before opening.** To know if a door is containing a fire in another room, touch the door. If it's hot, go to another exit. Opening the door will allow the fire to spread more quickly. Also teach your child to close all doors behind him as he leaves a fire zone.

**Never run back into a burning building.** Children, especially around the ages of five and six, often feel compelled to rescue others or to retrieve valued belongings once they have exited from a fire. Instill in your child the rule that once he has gotten out, he is to stay out.

**Know what a firefighter in full gear looks like.** When seeing a firefighter in full gear, many children panic at the mask and the tools—such as an ax—that a firefighter carries. Arrange with your child's school to have a full-dressed firefighter visit the class so that children are prepared to recognize a firefighter as a helper and not be tempted to try to get away should they ever encounter a firefighter. Or take your child to the local firehouse and ask the firefighters if you could see a display of uniforms and equipment.

Kitchen and bath accidents account for a number of burn injuries, too. Five- and six-year-olds are not mature enough to operate any cooking devices, even a microwave oven. The hot water heater's thermostat should be set to no more than 120 degrees Fahrenheit, and bathwater should not be above 100 degrees Fahrenheit.

## Playground injuries

Each year in the United States, more than 200,000 children are treated in emergency rooms for injuries received on the playground. Most injuries are the result of falls from swings, slides, see-saws, and climbing bars. To prevent injury, allow your child to play on such equipment only in areas that have soft ground surfaces. A 12-inch depth of wood chips, mulch, sand, or gravel or a 4-inch-thick carpet of rubber or other forgiving material can prevent serious harm. Also teach your child to use playground equipment properly; for instance, your child should never swing an empty swing toward another child, and he should test metal surfaces with his finger on hot days before sitting down on a slide that may be hot enough to cause a burn.

## Sports safety

If a sport involves wheels, blades, or skis, your child must wear an appropriate helmet before participating. Additional equipment, such as wrist and elbow pads, can also drastically lower the risk of injury.

If your child is involved in a team sport, make sure that the equipment used is the right size and in good condition. Large pieces of equipment, such as soccer goals, need to be adequately anchored to prevent tipping. Coaches should be well trained and concerned about safety. Five- and six-year-olds are not physically or emotionally mature enough to deal with sports activities that emphasize winning, and a team sport that does so risks endangering your child. The focus needs to be on fun and sportsmanship.

# ⬛ SAFETY FIRST
## Clothing hazards

Drawstrings, hoods, loose clothing, scarves, and dangling belts or sashes can cause injuries if these items catch on bedposts, in car doors, or on playground equipment. Remove drawstrings (or cut them so that no more than three inches dangle) and where possible, it is preferable to have your child wear hoodless sweatshirts and jackets.

---

Young players also need protection from the elements. Playing in the hot sun can cause heatstroke, sunburn, and dehydration. Be sure your child drinks plenty of water during any active playing.

### Appliances, tools, and lawnmowers

Your five- or six-year-old is eager to help out around the house, though he'll much prefer to work on jobs that are meant for bigger kids than to complete the usual tasks of picking up his toys and sorting socks.

Though your child is old enough to start to use some hand tools such as a hammer or screwdriver, he should never be permitted to handle any power tools. His maturity has not yet reached the stage where he can be counted on to stay as focused as he needs to be.

In the kitchen, your child can help prepare a salad, wash fruit, and make sandwiches, but he should never handle electrical appliances without very close supervision. For instance, your child might enjoy using an electric mixer to make frosting, but you should be standing at his side as he does so. (If your child has long hair, tie it back.) Always remind your child to stay away from water when using electrical items. And never let a five- or six-year-old use the stove, microwave, or other heat-producing appliance.

Lawnmowers pose a particular hazard to young children, and no child under the age of 12 should be permitted to operate a power mower or to ride, even accompanied by an adult, on a riding mower.

## Bunk beds

Your five- or six-year-old is likely to view the acquisition of a bunk bed as a major symbol of growing up. Though six is generally considered the earliest that most kids are ready, some larger and more mature fives can safely take their position on the top bunk.

If you do use a bunk bed, position it away from windows in the corner of the room, where the two walls will act as additional bracing for the bed. The following safety precautions should be followed:

*Make sure the mattress fits snugly.* There also should be two or more supports below the top mattress. The upper mattress should not be able to tip or move in any way that could cause it to fall onto the lower bunk.

*Install guardrails on the top bunk.* Secure guardrails along both long sides of the bed with screws or nails. The gap between the side rail and the guardrail should be no more than 3½ inches. Be sure your child can't roll under the guardrail when his weight compresses the mattress.

*Regularly check hardware.* Check the welds on metal frames and the screws on metal or wood frames.

*Teach bunk safety.* Have your child use a ladder to reach the top bunk. Don't allow more than one child on the top bunk at a time. Forbid horseplay, such as jumping from the bunk. Use a nightlight in case the child in the top bunk needs to get down in the middle of the night.

## Firearms

The level of coordination required to pull a trigger doesn't usually come until about age five—a time when your child is still very much caught up in fantasy play and too young to learn meaningful gun safety.

It's best not to have any firearms in a home with children. Nearly 200 American children a year are killed in their homes by playing with guns. (A firearm in the home is 43 times more likely to kill or injure a family member or visitor than to be used for protection against an intruder.) Surveys show that nearly 61 percent of gun owners with children in the home stored at least one gun in an accessible area. Fifteen percent of gun-owning families keep a loaded gun where children can get it, and some parents, who believe a gun is unloaded, have failed to check the firing chamber, where one bullet can be fatal. If you feel you must have a gun, keep it away from your child. The gun should always be locked up, and ammunition should be stored in a separate, locked area.

Parents who do not keep guns in their homes cannot assume that their child will not come into contact with a gun at the home of a friend or relative. Get in the habit of asking if firearms are in the home and, if so, if they are stored safely, before allowing your child to play in others' homes. Teach your child never to touch a gun and to leave the area and tell a grown-up immediately if a friend is playing with a gun.

## YOU AND YOUR CHILD
# Keeping your child safe without being overprotective

Parents of five- and six-year-olds often waver between wanting to envelop their children in cocoons, where they cannot get a chance to try their wings, and assuming that their children are more capable of taking care of themselves than they really are.

To help yourself judge if you're overprotective or if you're allowing more freedom of movement and expecting more responsibility than your child can comfortably handle, observe what your child's peers are doing. If yours is the only child who still must hold your hand as you walk down the sidewalk or if you aren't even thinking about letting your child graduate to a two-wheeler, you may be holding on just a bit too tightly. If, on the other hand, no other kids your child's age have the same range of freedom or the same level of responsibility at home, such as walking to school by himself, it's time to question your rules. Maybe your child really does need a bit more supervision than he's getting. Maybe he's doing things now that would be more appropriate in a year or two.

If your child is prodding you to allow more freedom, he may very well be ready for it. If his personality is more clingy, it may be up to you to do the prodding, to help him reach the same level of activity that his peers enjoy. Between the ages of five and six, your child really is ready to move on somewhat. Teaching him rules of safety goes a long way toward protecting him. He's just not ready to take on the whole job of keeping himself safe yet.

### Teaching your child about "stranger danger"

Teaching your child that the world is generally a safe and welcoming place gives him the courage to meet the challenges that he must, head on. You also need, of course, to teach him the boundaries of safety. One of the things that parents worry most about, although statistically it is very far down the list of real dangers, is abduction and harm of their child by a stranger. It's important that you teach your child never, ever to go off with anyone, even a well-known neighbor, without your knowledge. But it's also possible to overstate the danger and make your child fearful of everyone he meets. Also, statistically, your child is far more likely to be sexually or otherwise abused by someone he knows than by a stranger. So the real lesson you need to teach is not "stranger danger" but alertness to his own feelings and to actions by others that make him feel uncomfortable.

The key to keeping your child safe from abuse is to keep the lines of communication wide open. Tell your child repeatedly that he can tell you if someone he knows touches him inappropriately or asks him to keep secrets from you. Remind him that adults who scare children or ask them to do anything that makes them feel uneasy need to be reported to you. If your child ever does tell you about someone who has made him feel uncomfortable, even if it's someone you thoroughly trust, hear your child out and believe him. Then take the necessary action to keep your child safe and to alert the authorities so that no other child is at risk.

## Dealing with bullies

Being bullied can make an outgoing, happy child feel small and vulnerable. A child who bullies also feels out of control and seeks to repair the damage he feels in himself by overtaking another child. If your child is the victim of a bully:

***Be sure he feels free to tell you and his teachers.*** If a child is being picked on by another, it's not a good idea to tell him to stand up to the bully alone. (If he'd been able to do that, the bullying would not have continued.)

***Teach your child ways to diffuse a situation.*** He can walk away. He can join another group of nonaggressive kids. He can tell an adult. He can use humor. He can try to involve the bully on a more friendly basis. For instance, if a bully takes away his basketball, instead of appearing upset, he can say something like, "Instead of taking the ball, let's just play with it together."

***Help him form friendships with others who are not bullies.*** Being part of a larger group can insulate your child against bullying behavior.

***Role-play.*** Teach your child nonviolent responses to a bully. Let him practice his confident voice with you. Show him how to look a bully in the eye rather than sheepishly lowering his head. While never blaming your child for being a victim of a bully, observe him to see what behaviors of his might target him for bullying. Does he cry a bit too easily? Is he bragging? Is he acting aggressively himself? Is he making fun of the other child? Help him see the connection between his own behavior and that of the bully.

If your child is a bully, realize that he, too, suffers from bullying. Bullies are usually insecure and use their brawn instead of appropriate social skills to gain other children's attention. To help your child refrain from bullying behavior:

*Do not bully him.* Children who are frightened of their parents and who don't feel free to talk to them about their fears are far more likely to lash out at others.

*Develop positive strategies for dealing with frustration.* Teach your child to use words instead of his fists to express himself.

*Encourage feelings of empathy.* Help him understand how others feel when he bullies.

*Monitor his role models.* Your child may be overexposed to images of "heroes" getting their way or solving problems through violence. Help him see that there are better ways.

*Consult with school officials.* Many school districts have programs that teach children mediation skills.

## HELPING YOUR CHILD GROW
## Teaching safety rules

Since your child was old enough to understand, you probably focused greatly on safety in all everyday interactions. At this age, it's still largely up to you to keep your child safe, but beyond the specific rules for different occasions (helmets for bike riding, no diving in the shallow end of a pool) there are general rules that you need to be sure your child knows now:

*His first and last name, his address, and his phone number.* Make sure your child has memorized this information. When you're traveling, always tuck a piece of paper in his pocket that includes the name, address, and phone number of where you're staying, and make sure your child knows the hotel's name.

***Always to let you know where he is.*** Make sure your child is in the habit of checking in with you when you're outdoors. If he wants to move from the swing area of the playground to the slides a half-a-block away, he needs to tell you.

***How to dial 911.*** By five, your child is ready to learn how to call for help if you become disabled or injured, or if he becomes lost. Using a toy phone, rehearse what to do and what to say.

**A *plan in case he gets lost*.** Most kids, at some time or another, become separated from their parents in stores or at amusement parks. Having a plan can mean the difference between a long, frightening separation and a quick reunion. When entering a building, always remind your child never to exit without you. In a store, theater, or large restaurant, find a landmark, such as the cash register, where you will meet if separated. Point out uniformed guards or other potential helpers, such as cashiers, to whom your child can turn for help. If on the street, teach your child a consistent rule, such as calling 911, stepping into a store that displays a "Safe Haven" or other such ID that marks it as a place where children can go for help, staying put and waiting for you, or asking a mom with kids for assistance. Review the plan before outings in a matter-of-fact way.

---

# Respect your child's uniqueness

All children develop intellectually and emotionally at their own pace. It's your job to support and encourage your child's own schedule—and enjoy this magic stage!

# The best books

Your five- and six-year-old has entered a world of books as never before. Now, he not only looks forward to listening to you read to him, but he's taking on the task of choosing and reading books on his own. No doubt, his teacher and the school librarian will have many suggestions to further his reading. You can also suggest these classics—old and new:

- *Bedhead* by Margie Palatini (Simon & Schuster). A hilarious look at a girl suffering from a *really* bad hair day—perfect for kids who are just becoming aware of how they appear to others.
- *Bedtime for Frances* by Russel Hoban (HarperTrophy). One of the series about a delightful badger.
- *Buzz* by Janet S. Wong (Harcourt Brace). Kids with working parents will identify with this story's busy and loving family.
- *Eloise* by Kay Thompson (Simon & Schuster). The story of a six-year-old who makes her home at the Plaza Hotel in New York will entrance your six-year old.
- *Emily's First 100 Days of School* by Rosemary Wells (Hyperion Press). A wonderful recounting of school activities with a fun lesson on counting to 100.
- *Goldilocks and the Three Bears: A Tale Moderne* by Steven Guarnaccia (Harry N. Abrams). Children who are familiar with the classic Goldilocks tale will enjoy this modern twist.
- *Junie B. Jones Has a Peep in Her Pocket* by Barbara Park (Random House). This is number 15 in a series about Junie B. Jones, also known as "the world's funniest kindergartner."
- *Sylvester and the Magic Pebble* by William Steig (Aladdin Paperbacks). This tale of Sylvester who makes an ill-conceived wish will capture your child's imagination.

# The best videos

Video releases of recently seen movies along with classic Disney and pop-character films are apt to be your child's favorites now. In addition to current blockbusters, consider these films, which you'll enjoy watching along with your child:

- *Annie.* The cartoon-come-to-life story of a little orphan girl who finds a family.
- *Home Alone.* When his family takes off for vacation without him, a young boy must defend his home by himself.
- *It's the Great Pumpkin, Charlie Brown* (Peanuts Classic). This story of faith and hope has won fans for generations.
- *Mary Poppins* (Walt Disney Gold Collection). A technologically-advanced story of a family's search for the perfect nanny.
- *My Neighbor Totoro* (Fox Video Family Feature). The story of a Japanese girl who must adapt from rural to city life.
- *Paulie.* The story of a parrot who longs for home and the child who loved him.
- *Willy Wonka and the Chocolate Factory.* Based on Roald Dahl's classic book, this film will likely become a favorite.

# The best computer programs

These programs provide fun and learning that's just right for kindergartners and first graders:

- *Arthur's Computer Adventure* (Creative Wonders) Win/Mac.
- *Backyard Baseball* (Humongous Entertainment) Win/Mac.
- *Backyard Football* (Humongous Entertainment) Win/Mac.
- *Disney's Ready to Read with Pooh* (Disney Interactive) Win/Mac.
- *Disney's Winnie the Pooh Kindergarten* (Disney Interactive) Win/Mac.
- *Jump Start Kindergarten* (Knowledge Adventure) Win/Mac.
- *Jump Start 1st Grade* (Knowledge Adventure) Win/Mac.
- *KidPix Studio Deluxe* (Broderbund/Mindscape) Win/Mac.
- *Math Blaster for 1st Grade* (Knowledge Adventure) Win/Mac.
- *Mercer Mayer's Just Me and My Mom* series (Humongous Entertainment) Win/Mac.
- *Reader Rabbit Thinking Adventures Ages 4–6* (The Learning Company) Win/Mac.
- *Scholastic's The Magic School Bus* series (Microsoft) Win.
- *Tonka Construction* (Hasbro Interactive) Win/Mac.
- *Tonka Construction 2* (Hasbro Interactive) Win.